D1530346

FLY NOW!

FLY NOW!

A COLORFUL STORY OF FLIGHT FROM HOT AIR BALLOON TO THE 777 "WORLDLINER"

THE POSTER COLLECTION OF THE SMITHSONIAN NATIONAL AIR AND SPACE MUSEUM

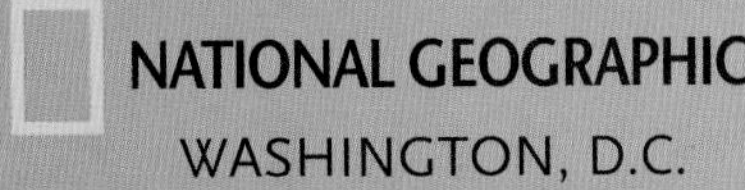
NATIONAL GEOGRAPHIC
WASHINGTON, D.C.

Oh -
let us fly
— but *do* let it be with the
Dutch-Swedish Air Line

AEROTRANSPORT Swedish Air Lines

&

K L M Royal Dutch Air Lines

Information and Air-tickets here!

CONTENTS

OH—LET US FLY
CIRCA 1939
39 x 24 1/2 in.

FOREWORD

BY HERB KELLEHER

CO-FOUNDER AND EXECUTIVE CHAIRMAN, SOUTHWEST AIRLINES

Go. See. Do. But at all times, *Be Yourself.*

This is advice that I have followed throughout my career. In 1967, when Rollin King and I formed Southwest Airlines, our intention was to create an airline to fit the Texas intrastate market. When the domestic airline industry was deregulated in 1978, we could have tried to become like the traditional air carriers. Instead, we decided to stick with our original business plan, and fly short hops, point-to-point, as frequently and as cheaply as possible. We turned what appeared to be a weakness into a strategic and operational strength. Embracing paradox is one way to define Southwest's business plan, and our advertising reflects it. While we hope our print ads and television spots speak to potential passengers, we know they accurately portray Southwest's personality and style—work hard, but have fun.

The posters in *Fly Now!*, all selected from the poster collection of the Smithsonian National Air and Space Museum, give us insight into how the aviation industry has defined itself from balloons in 1827 to the present. When first selling their wares to the public, many aeronauts and then aviators were content to depict themselves as circus-like entertainers and their flying as a performance. Once airlines began to sell seats, companies quickly realized that they were going to have to forge a new public identity for aviation—disassociating it from the whimsy and aimlessness of ballooning and aviation expositions. But how were they to tell travelers that flying was the way to go, how were they going to gain passengers' loyalty, and how would they describe themselves? "Are we the safe, secure, comfortable, reliable airline?" "Are we the company that always flies the newest aircraft?" "Do we use avant-garde artists or commission only realistic imagery?" By contrast, after World War II, the world was sufficiently air-minded that airlines stopped worrying about selling the idea of flight and instead depicted themselves as "transformers": Climb aboard, and we'll make you feel like a jet-setter, James Bond, a Hollywood starlet, an international traveler, Hugh Hefner. Snap your fingers, and we will take you "there."

For someone interested in entrepreneurship, *Fly Now!*'s look into aviation's past—a veritable parade of start-up companies—is fascinating. The book goes right to the crux of the issue, asking the question, "Why fly in the first place?" This quirky, colorful look at how aeronauts and airlines answered that question will entertain you, amuse you, and with any luck make you reflect on the significance of aviation in your life.

GO SEE DO
CIRCA 1999
28 x 22 in.

INTRODUCTION

BY F. ROBERT VAN DER LINDEN

CURATOR OF AIR TRANSPORTATION, NATIONAL AIR AND SPACE MUSEUM

For more than two centuries human flight has fired the imagination with its compelling visions of escape from an earth-bound existence. After the Montgolfier brothers took to the skies of Paris by balloon in 1783, flight became a possibility to which all might aspire. For generations, flight has symbolized freedom and progress, whether real or imagined, and unlimited possibilities of new technology. Powered, controlled, heavier-than-air flight was a dominant technology of the 20th century. While the balloon traveled with the caprices of the wind, the airplane went wherever the pilot wished. The genius of Wilbur and Orville Wright, and that of the countless other engineers, designers, and visionaries who followed, allowed humankind to explore the world on a different scale, unleashing the potential of their remarkable invention.

First a novelty at fairs and sideshows, aviation expanded its roles as breakthroughs in structures, aerodynamics, design, and propulsion made the airplane increasingly useful. One decade after the Wrights flew at Kitty Hawk, North Carolina, in 1903, the airplane had become an indispensable weapon that dominated 20th century conflict. The airplane is largely responsible for the expansion of total warfare.

But in another way the airplane has far exceeded the dreams of its creators. As early as 1914, the first scheduled airline carried passengers across Tampa Bay, Florida. The St. Petersburg-Tampa Air Boat Line was a small but critical step toward a huge international industry employing thousands of people and transporting billions. Virtually anywhere on the planet is accessible within one day's travel time. The social, economic, and political impact is huge as geographical obstacles no longer exist. The airplane has transformed the world.

The history of aviation has been traced well in books and articles. Joanne Gernstein London's fascinating interpretation of aviation through that of a different media—posters—reveals new insights on this oft'-told story and provides a richness of interpretation and analysis that staid histories cannot convey. In this exciting account, Dr. London follows the exploits of early balloonists and their attempts to capitalize financially on their deeds. Images of aviation were used by governments to gain popular support of wars, and posters promoted the airplane as a symbol of progress. By far the most powerful posters are those promoting aerial travel. Dr. London traces the evolution of the airline industry through the often stunningly beautiful works that first sought to convince the public of the safety and utility of flight. Later, once the aircraft had become an accepted medium of transportation, posters enticed travelers to exotic destinations. Throughout, Dr. London portrays the airplane as a fast, safe, exciting means of travel—as an adventure, and as an aspiration for the uninitiated.

I am pleased that this important work will accompany the opening of a new exhibition in the National Air and Space Museum in 2007. Entitled "America by Air," this exhibit will trace the fascinating history of America's airline industry and its profound effect upon the nation and the world. Highlighted throughout will be airline posters, many included in this book. They gracefully accent each period and complement the dozens of other artifacts ranging from the smallest baggage label to a massive Boeing 747 nose section. They lend color and a sense of time and place to the compelling story of air travel.

INTRODUCTION

BY JOANNE GERNSTEIN LONDON

CURATOR, AERONAUTICS DIVISION, NATIONAL AIR AND SPACE MUSEUM

In 1968 my parents went searching for a London Underground poster they had seen while traveling on the Tube. Eventually they made their way to the London Transport office. At that dreary and utilitarian place, they purchased several striking airline posters; one still hangs in their apartment in St. Louis.

My parents' delight in traveling and their propensity to bring back posters set the stage for my interest in aviation history. When I arrived at the National Air and Space Museum (NASM) in 1987, to work on the museum's new WWI gallery, I had flown on many airplanes, but had read little about them. I began my aeronautical education while working on World War I- and World War II-themed exhibitions. Then, I started to curate—to catalog, organize, house, and research—the NASM's poster collection. Although the 1,000 posters had been in the museum's possession for decades, they had garnered little attention. The prospect of organizing them into a meaningful collection intrigued me. I could see that these beautiful pieces would reveal an important but untold story of aviation—namely, how aviation had been sold through advertising, from early balloons to modern jets.

As I began gathering each poster's vital statistics—such as descriptions of its imagery and dimensions—to enter into an artifact database, I started to see themes and patterns in these advertisements. But few had dates—and dates were critical to the story. So I searched through contemporary timetable collections, aviation journals, newspapers, and scholarly articles on the geography, economics, or politics of aeronautics. Eventually I determined a date for each poster, and in the process I gained insight into the marketing rationale that created it.

In choosing posters for *Fly Now!* from the collection's now 1,400 artifacts, I focused on what I see as the collection's main story: the development of commercial aviation. The posters particularly illustrate the aviation community's efforts to advertise itself through 19th-century ballooning exhibition posters, through early 20th-century airplane exhibition and meet posters, and most of all, through airline advertisements from the period between WWI and WWII. The wars themselves are little represented in the posters, but the wars cannot be neglected. In selecting posters for each chapter, I chose those with the most brilliant imagery and the most interesting histories of commercial aviation; many also gave insight into how the world wars affected the airline industry. I ended the book in 1978, the year the U.S. airline industry was deregulated—when the government transferred to the airlines the responsibility for setting fares and routes. This ended a chapter in the story of commercial aviation—and began a new one. The effusive posters of early commercial growth are gone. Airline marketing budgets today rely more on radio, television, and internet. But posters still play a role, and I am collecting posters to tell that story.

I hope that after traveling through the pages of *Fly Now!* readers from aviation enthusiasts to those not yet airminded will bring home a new regard for aviation and a refreshed view about the role air travel plays in their everyday lives.

SQUARE DES BATIGNOLLES

FÊTE DE L'ŒUVRE DES LOYERS

DU XVIIme ARRONDISSEMENT

DIMANCHE
4 Juillet 1886

FÊTE
DE
JOUR

Prix d'Entrée :
1 fr.

COURSES A PIED
—
THEATRE-CONCERT
—
COURSES A ANE
—
BAL D'ENFANTS
—
EXPERIENCES TELEPHONIQUES
—
CONCERT MILITAIRE

A 5 HEURES 1/2
Ascension du Ballon
SOUS LA
Présidence de
PAR LES
Louis GODARD &
Qui exécuteront à 7 et 10
LES EXERCICES

LOUIS GODARD

DIMANCHE
4 Juillet 1886

FÊTE
DE
NUIT

Prix d'Entrée :
1 fr.

Théâtre-Concert
—
GRAND BAL DE NUIT
—
ILLUMINATIONS
VÉNITIENNES
—
ECLAIRAGE ELECTRIQUE PAR ACCUMULATEURS
—
RETRAITE AUX FLAMBEAUX

L'ŒUVRE DES LOYERS
M. GABRIEL YON
AÉRONAUTES
CAPITAINE JULHÈS
mètres au-dessous de la nacelle
DU DOUBLE TRAPÈZE

CHAPTER ONE

UP THERE, LOOK!

1783–1911

The industrial revolution, most often associated with iron and steel, was also known for lighter-than-air experimentation. From the mid-1700s, British inventors building with steel, iron, and other new materials, devised machines and manufacturing processes at an unprecedented rate. British chemists discovered the differences between gases such as oxygen and hydrogen. Applying these new ideas, Joseph Montgolfier and his brother Etienne built and flew the world's first hot-air balloon in the summer of 1783. Crowds gathered to watch them and by the end of that year other balloonists had joined them in the skies over Europe and the United States.

By the early 1800s, balloon ascensions were no longer novel. Eager to maintain public interest, balloonists added exotic attractions to their shows. Posters promised ticket holders views of North American Osage Indians floating aloft or scantily clad women dangling by their hair from a balloon's basket. Paying passengers were taking their first

GODARD
1886
48 1/2 x 32 in.

balloon rides in the 1830s. By the 1890s, excitement over balloon ascensions was fading. Yet, as ballooning was losing popular appeal, it was being taken up by wealthy sportsmen. Aeronauts Louis Godard and Gabriel Yon profited handsomely from this shift in clientele, provisioning well-to-do amateurs all over the world from their Paris factory from 1895 until the start of World War I in 1914.

But ballooning did not present enough challenge for long. Soon the amateurs, who had abandoned infatuations with autos to fly balloons, switched to airplanes. The Wright brothers had made the first controlled heavier-than-air flight in 1903; by 1909 flying burgeoned as a sport—an expensive one. Some pilots without funds, like Alys McKey in the poster at right, performed with exhibition companies in order to have access to airplanes and to make money to fly more.

Most often daredevils from birth *and* mechanically inclined, early pilots like McKey and her counterparts worldwide flew competitively to fund their flying habits. When companies, wealthy entrepreneurs, or military establishments put up prize money, pilots followed. From the Country Club Grounds in Portland, Oregon, to new airfields in southern France, the name of the game was record-making.

In 1913 Alys McKey set altitude records and took the title "First Female Pilot to Fly in . . ." Idaho, Oregon, Washington State, and

Alys McKey, known in the popular press as "The Birdwoman," made her name flying in spectacular air shows and later made her mark in aviation history training pilots during World War I.

Canada. Many pilots, including Alys's husband, noted barnstormer Milton Bryant, who died in a crash in 1913, made their last flights attempting to be first. Like extreme sports today, death-defying acts added a compelling—if macabre—element for spectators.

Into the early 20th century, promoters of ballooning extravaganzas and aerial exhibitions commissioned posters they hoped would stand out on the hoardings, where advertisements were displayed. The posters sold an exciting intangible—a vicarious relationship with aeronauts and pilots, celebrities of the industrial revolution.

ALYS MCKEY
1913
14 1/4 x 22 in.

TIVOLI,

Rue de Clichy, n° 80, Pavillon Labouxière.

Demain DIMANCHE 14 Octobre 1827,

PA EXT AORDINAIRE

Grande Fête

A laquelle assisteront

LES OSAGES

A 4 heures précises, ASCENSION EN BALLON par M. D.-DELCOURT.

Les *OSAGES* seront promenés à *BALLON CAPTIF* dans l'enceinte de Tivoli, si le temps le permet.

L'affiche du jour indiquera les détails.

Prix d'Entrée : TROIS fr. par personne.

TIVOLI
1827
15 x 25 in.

EVERYONE A VOYEUR

The designer of the poster at left hoped that "TIVOLI" and "LES OSAGES" set in large type would stop pedestrians in their tracks. The original Tivoli Garden, great-grandfather of modern-day amusement parks, opened in Paris in 1795. Until it closed in 1825, Tivoli was popular with fashionable Parisians. Even after the park's demise, the French continued to associate the name "Tivoli" with spectacle, excitement, leisure, and decadence. When Belgian balloonist Etienne-Gaspart Robert (known to crowds as Robertson) opened his balloon park in 1826 farther north along the Rue de Clichy, he named it Tivoli. Robertson, presumably the sponsor of the poster, also borrowed the format of original Tivoli Garden advertisements to publicize his new park.

The small group of Osage Indians featured at the "Grande Fête" had traveled from their home in Missouri to France to visit French "friends" who had been their trading partners in North America. Only six journeyed to Le Havre, France, in July 1827, but they made a big impression. Seeing and being seen with the Osage delegation was a status symbol, sought by bourgeoisie and royalty alike. The Osages's hosts introduced them to such celebrated institutions as French opera, King Charles X, and ballooning.

RÉPUBLIQUE FRANÇAISE

ARGENTEUIL

FÊTES DE LA PENTECOTE

Dimanche 13, Lundi 14, Mardi 15 et Dimanche 20 Juin 1886

Sur les magnifiques promenades de la ville dont les ombrages s'étendent sur plus d'un kilomètre le long de la Seine

DIMANCHE 13 JUIN

SALVES

d'Artillerie

RÉGATES

JEUX DIVERS

Théâtres, Cirques
Ménagerie
Musée du Divorce

ILLUMINATIONS

ANNAMITES

DIMANCHE 13 JUIN

CONCERT

Instrumental

PAR LA

Fanfare Municipale

à 3 heures

GRAND BAL

Musée, Aquarium

ILLUMINATIONS

ANNAMITES

LUNDI 14 JUIN, A 4 HEURES TRÈS PRÉCISES

ENLEVEMENT DU BALLON

LE PARMENTIER

Lundi 14 Juin, à 3 heures

CAVALCADE AÉRIENNE

AU DÉPART: Pluie de fleurs, pommes de terre frites, bonbons, jouets, etc.

A 400 mètres

Lâcher de Pigeons voyageurs

Mardi 15 Juin, à 2 heures (prix nombreux)

Pour les Filles

A 3 heures

Pour les Garçons

NOUVELLES
ILLUMINATIONS

Dimanche 20 Juin, à 2 heures

GRAND

FESTIVAL

de Musique Instrumentale

RÉCOMPENSES: PALMES, MÉDAILLES D'OR, ETC.

A 3 heures (prix divers)

COURSES INTERNATIONALES
de Culs-de-Jatte

A 9 heures

RETRAITE ÉGYPTIENNE

FEU D'ARTIFICE

Illuminations générales des Promenades

Cortège immense des Sociétés Musicales, de Gymnastique, des Sapeurs-Pompiers, etc.

GRAND BAL DE NUIT

Sous la tente WILLIS

Les Commissaires de la Fête: MM. POTHRON, Adjoint; Alexandre RENARD, GIRARDIN-COLLAS, ROULAND, SENÉCHAL, DUBOIS, BRAQUE, LABRIERRE.

Le Maire, G. DANTIER

MOYENS DE TRANSPORT: Départ de la gare Saint-Lazare, toutes les heures 5 minutes; gare du Nord, toutes les heures 33 minutes. — Des trains supplémentaires seront organisés suivant les besoins du service.

Argenteuil. — P. WORMS, imprimeur breveté, rue de la Chaussée, 4

BALLOON ASCENSIONS

AERONAUTS MADE BALLOON ASCENSIONS IN A VARIETY OF PUBLIC SPACES, from festival grounds to city squares. In Argenteuil, a suburb of Paris and favorite weekend destination for middle-class Parisians, festival organizers introduced the balloon *enlevement* (meaning "ascension") to enliven the usual tourist attractions of their city.

Festivals remained a constant in French life even after their purpose as religious spectacles waned. For centuries, Pentecost celebrations at Argenteuil had signified the important role of the church in community and everyday life. But 19th-century modernization strengthened the link between villages and Paris—and drastically changed citizens' mental maps of their world. A new web of economic interdependence led many to question traditional values. Interest in technology and an anticlerical movement transformed centuries-old religious festivals into just another form of urban entertainment.

With this new outlook, aeronauts in the late 1880s pledged their lives to the pursuit of science and the reform of the public's image of balloonists as hucksters. Still, the best-known balloonists were the popular performers—like Francois Lhoste, featured at left. Lhoste made the first cross-Channel flight from France in 1883. He repeated the feat twice more to prove that skill, not luck, had brought him success. Upon his death in 1887, the editor of the *Revue de l'Aeronautique* argued that despite Lhoste's celebrity, he still warranted praise in the hallowed publication for his scientific contribution.

ARGENTEUIL
1886
48 1/2 x 33 1/2 in.

DARING ACROBATS

ALTHOUGH LITTLE IS KNOWN ABOUT MISS STENA, SHOWN DANGLING BY HER hair at right, the design of the poster is characteristic of late 19th-century French circus advertisements, which used imagery to showcase female performers' daring acts and daring costumes and attract customers.

While demure by 21st-century standards, Miss Stena's low-cut, ruffled neckline, short skirt, and red boots were risqué to circus-goers who came dressed in clothes that covered them from head to toe. Nineteenth-century painters used the relationship between circus performers and their audiences to examine attitudes about the body, personal space, and public presentations of self. In contrast to the poster's dominant image of the skimpily clad Miss Stena, the balloon inset shows her wearing earrings (perhaps pearl) and a cameo necklace, with a stylish depiction of possibly the star's own face. The portrait suggests that, offstage, Miss Stena possessed all the accoutrements of a well-dressed, or at least well-kept, woman of her time. The poster's two depictions of Miss Stena, as daring acrobat and conventionally dressed woman, may have piqued the interests of upper-class patrons and lured them to her performances.

Ballooning, like circus life, ran in families. Jeanne-Geneviève Labrosse, the first woman to pilot a balloon in 1798 and use a parachute to descend from her craft in 1799, married parachute inventor and aeronaut Jacques Garnerin. Her niece Elisa Garnerin specialized in pinpoint parachute landings from a balloon basket.

MISS STENA
CIRCA 1890
21 1/8 x 17 1/4 in.

DESCENTE D'ABSALON
Par Miss Stena
Faddegon & Co Lith. Amst. (Holland)

САДЪ КОНЦЕРТОВЪ АРБАНА.

У Измайловскаго моста, по фонтанкѣ, домъ Гг. Тарасовыхъ, (бывшее лѣтнее помѣщеніе Нѣмецкаго клуба).

ВЪ СУББОТУ, 30 АВГУСТА,

НЕ ВЪ СЧЕТЪ АБОНЕМЕНТА

БОЛЬШОЕ ПРЕДСТАВЛЕНІЕ

СЪ ПОЛНОЮ ГАЗАВОЮ ИЛЛЮМИНАЦІЕЮ

И

ВОЗДУШНОЕ ПУТЕШЕСТВІЕ

ИЗВѢСТНАГО ВОЗДУХОПЛАВАТЕЛЯ

АЛЕКСАНДРА ШПЕРЛИНГА,

во вновь устроенномъ имъ колоссальномъ шарѣ подъ названіемъ:

„С.-ПЕТЕРБУРГЪ“.

Г-нъ Шперлингъ поднимется на воздухѣ въ гондолѣ, прикрѣпленной подъ шаромъ съ пассажиркою, заранѣе заявившею свое желаніе сопутствовать воздухоплавателю.

Во время наполненія шара будетъ пущено нѣсколько сигнальныхъ шаровъ для опредѣленія направленія большаго шара.

Когда шаръ достигнетъ извѣстной высоты, то воздухоплаватель пуститъ нѣсколько парашютовъ съ разными предметами.

Наполненіе шара водороднымъ газомъ изъ 40 большихъ бочекъ съ газометромъ начнется въ 4 часа вечера.

ПОДНЯТІЕ БОЛЬШОГО ШАРА „С.-ПЕТЕРБУРГЪ“ СЪ ВОЗДУХОПЛАВАТЕЛЕМЪ РОВНО ВЪ $6\frac{1}{2}$ ЧАСОВЪ ВЕЧЕРА.

ПОРЯДОКЪ ПРЕДСТАВЛЕНІЯ:

Съ 4-хъ до $6\frac{1}{2}$ часовъ вечера будетъ играть хоръ военной музыки 37-й дивизіи попеременно съ хоромъ пѣсенниковъ **Ивана Молчанова.**

По поднятіи шара начнется первое отдѣленіе на сценѣ.

Хоръ военной музыки исполнитъ три отдѣленія.

Въ антрактахъ играетъ хоръ военной музыки 37-й дивизіи.

Въ I отдѣленіи на сценѣ примутъ участіе: хоръ цыганъ, подъ управленіемъ извѣстнаго **Петра Васильева,** (въ этомъ хорѣ находятся слѣдующія солистки: **Марія, Татьяна, Ольга, Шишкина, Анна** и друг.), комики **Мартинеттъ,** хоръ венгерскихъ пѣвицъ и хоръ русскихъ пѣвцовъ **Молчанова.**

Во II отдѣленіи примутъ участіе: хоръ цыганъ подъ управленіемъ **Петра Васильева,** хоръ венгерскихъ пѣвицъ (солистки: **Корнелія Панъ, Элла Шрейнеръ, Роза Хорвальтъ, Марія Нотгардтъ, Дальноки** и друг.), комики **Мартинеттъ** и хоръ русскихъ пѣвцовъ **Молчанова.**

Въ III отдѣленіи хоръ военной музыки и хоръ московскихъ цыганъ.

Начало вечера въ 4 часа.

Цѣна за входъ 75 коп.

Для удобства публики около шара устроены мѣста съ платою: стулья по 1 руб., скамейки по 50 коп.

Контрамарки при выходѣ изъ сада не выдаются.

Въ случаѣ дождя иллюминація и полетъ воздушнаго шара съ воздухоплавателемъ отмѣняются, остальное же будетъ исполнено въ точности по программѣ.

Въ Воскресенье, 31 Августа, послѣдній музыкальный вечеръ, передъ закрытіемъ сада, съ участіемъ всѣхъ артистовъ.

В. Н. Егаревъ.

Печ. дозв. 27 Августа 1875 г. Спб. Градоначальникъ Генералъ-Адъютантъ Треповъ.

Въ тип. Императорскихъ Спб. театровъ (Эдуарда Гоппе) Вознес. просп., д. № 53. 4—6

18 75

С.-ПЕТЕРБУРГСКІЙ

ЗООЛОГИЧЕСКІЙ САДЪ.

Въ Александровскомъ паркѣ.

Сегодня, въ Субботу, 30-го Августа,

не въ счетъ абонемента,

БЕНЕФИСЪ

извѣстнаго неподражаемаго (человѣкъ рыба)

Г-на ОСКАРА ДЕБУРГЪ.

ИМѢЕТЪ БЫТЬ:

БОЛЬШОЕ ПРЕДСТАВЛЕНІЕ,

при двухъ оркестрахъ музыки, электрическимъ освѣщеніи и блистательной роскошной иллюминаціи всего сада, съ участіемъ полнаго состава артистовъ, дававшихъ свои представленія въ теченіи лѣтняго сезона сего года, въ заключеніе 2-го отдѣленія въ саду, на гимнастической сценѣ дана будетъ итальянская комическая пантомима:

„АРЛЕКИНЪ СКЕЛЕТЪ“.

Начало музыки въ 3 часа пополудни.

Начало представленія въ $6\frac{1}{2}$ часовъ вечера.

Кормленіе звѣрей въ 6 часовъ.

Цѣна за входъ 30 коп. съ персоны; дѣти до 10 лѣтъ 15 коп.

Садъ открытъ съ 10 часовъ утра.

Контрамарки при выходѣ изъ сада на обратный входъ не выдаются.

Э. РОСТЪ.

Печ. дозв. 28 Августа 1875 г. Спб. Градоначальникъ Генералъ-Адъютантъ Треповъ.

Въ тип. Императорскихъ Спб театровъ (Эдуарда Гоппе), Вознесенскій пр., д. № 53. 5—6

BALLOONS EVERYWHERE

Parisians lucky enough to take a balloon ride saw the culturally disparate arrondissements of Paris meld into one city. In Chicago, citizens hoped that balloon ascensions would put their hometown on the list of technologically advanced cities of the world. Saint Petersburg—the port city built in 1703 by Tsar Peter the Great as Russia's capital and "window on Europe"—had long been the home of the Russian Navy. In 1885, the Russian Army established a school for balloonists there.

Like other balloon ascensions around the world, the 1875 flight of *Pochta 2,* in the poster at left, took place during a weekend fair featuring military band concerts, gypsy singers, and fireworks. More serious events, however, were on the rise around the world. Changes in class structure, technology, communications, and aeronautics were challenging the status quo and redefining social and cultural boundaries in the U.S., Russia, and Europe. The prospect of war loomed on almost every continent. In 1874 France took the lead in establishing a formal military commission on ballooning. By the 1880s Russia and several major European powers had established military commissions, departments, or divisions to address the issue of fighting wars from the air.

2nd POCHTA
1875
32 1/2 x 19 1/2 in.

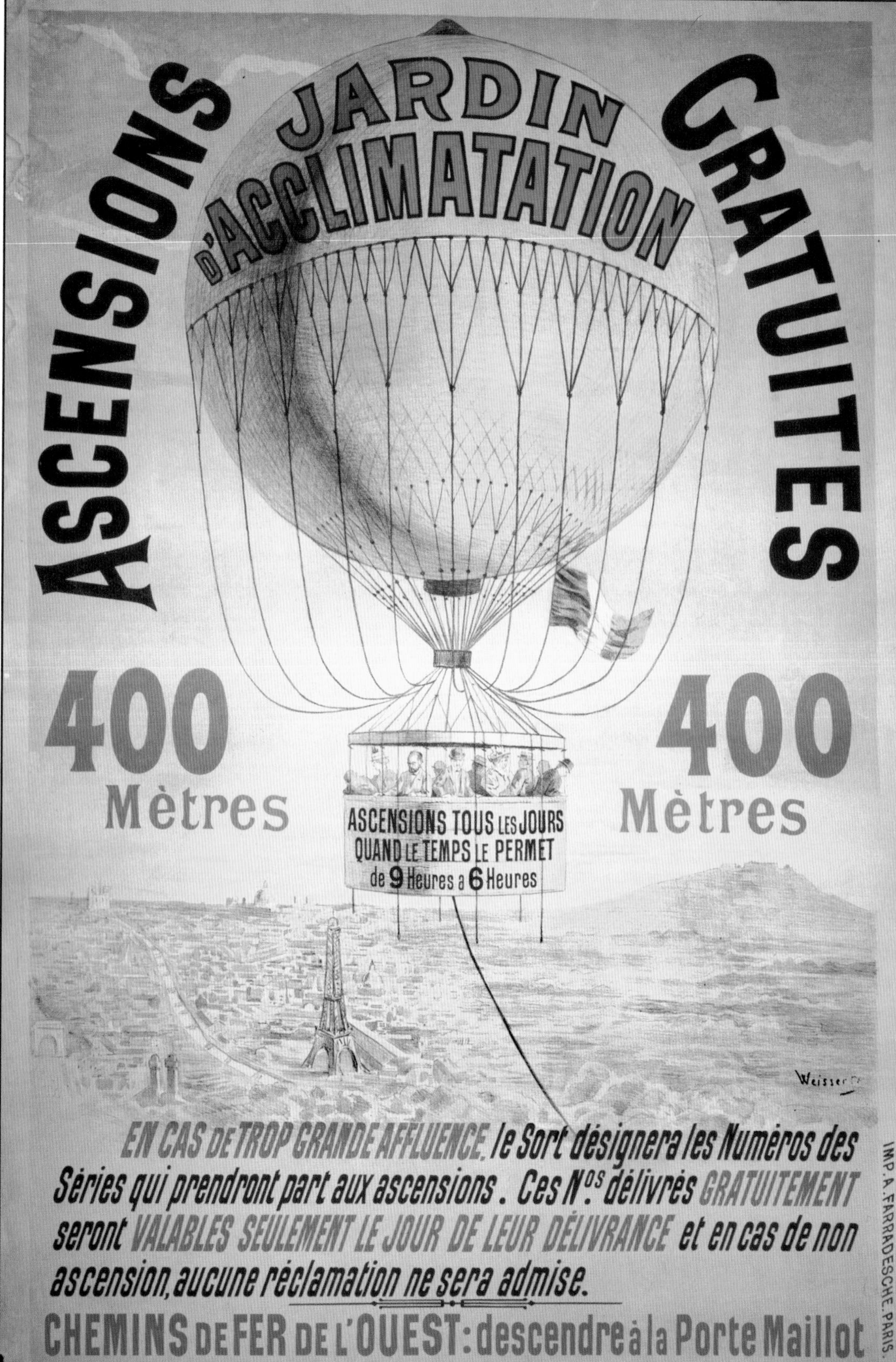
ASCENSIONS GRATUITES
JARDIN D'ACCLIMATATION
400 Mètres
400 Mètres
ASCENSIONS TOUS LES JOURS
QUAND LE TEMPS LE PERMET
de 9 Heures a 6 Heures
Weisser
EN CAS DE TROP GRANDE AFFLUENCE, le Sort désignera les Numéros des Séries qui prendront part aux ascensions. Ces N.os délivrés GRATUITEMENT seront VALABLES SEULEMENT LE JOUR DE LEUR DÉLIVRANCE et en cas de non ascension, aucune réclamation ne sera admise.
CHEMINS DE FER DE L'OUEST: descendre à la Porte Maillot
IMP. A. FARRADESCHE. PARIS.

AVIATION
COUPE PARIS-PA
GABARD

A CRADLE OF AVIATION

Where is Pau? To wealthy 19th-century Europeans, the mention of the small town conjured visions of a perennially sunny resort near the Pyrénées mountains. Among scientists, the majority of whom were drawn from the same elite class of people who wintered in Pau, the town was a research hub, especially associated with meteorology. This agreeable mix of wealth, scientific patronage, and, most of all, good weather convinced aviation pioneer Wilbur Wright to establish a flying school in Pau in 1908—just five years after he and brother Orville had made the world's first controlled flights. In early 1909, he taught his first three students. Thousands witnessed their training flights, including the kings of Spain and England.

The Wright brothers' school anointed Pau as France's first city of flight. In November 1909 Frenchman Louis Blériot, who had made a name piloting the first airplane across the English Channel on July 25, 1909, also started a flying school in Pau. By 1913 airplane companies Voisin, Antoinette, Deperdussin, Nieuport, Morane-Saulnier, in addition to dirigible builder Société Astra, had all launched flying schools in the vicinity of Pau.

The Pau-Aviation poster on the previous pages reflects this heritage. High above the city, aircraft float in an ethereal, bright yellow sky. Below, the solid shape of an eagle, native to the mountainous region south of Pau, flies low above the poster's big black letters. Artist Ernest Gabard's imagery suggests technology will prevail over nature, bringing humans closer to the heavens.

PREVIOUS PAGES: PAU
1911
28 1/2 x 44 1/2 in.

The poster captures the excitement that aviation engendered. Industrialists and organizations offered prizes to aviators who could fly highest, fastest, or farthest. In 1911 the Aéro Club of Béarn announced a $4,000 award to the aviator who made the fastest flight between Paris and Pau—a distance of some 500 miles. On April 24, 1911, Jules (aka Pierre) Védrine won the prize. He completed the flight in seven hours flying time—with three extended stops—during a three-day period. "Fast" for Védrine and his audience meant any speed surpassing that of the express train, whose top speed was clocked at 60 mph.

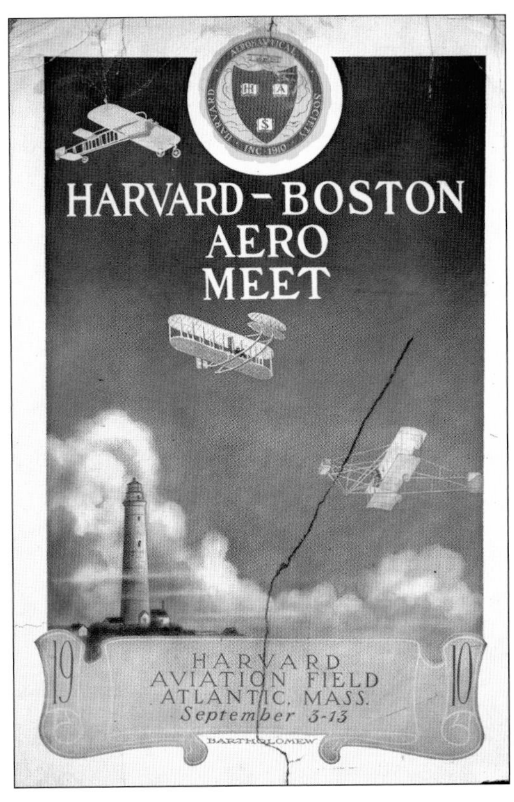

The city of Boston, the Aero Club of America, the Harvard Aeronautical Society, and U.S. aviators hoped the Harvard-Boston Aero Meet's $37,400 prize would attract record-setting pilots from around the world.

As political instability threatened Europe in 1911, the French minister of war turned to Pau. He ordered an airfield to be built there and installed the nation's First Aviation Regiment. The advent of World War I in 1914 further elevated Pau's status as a cradle of aviation. Almost every French World War I ace had earned his wings in Pau's blue sky.

HARVARD-BOSTON
1910
20 1/2 x 14 in.

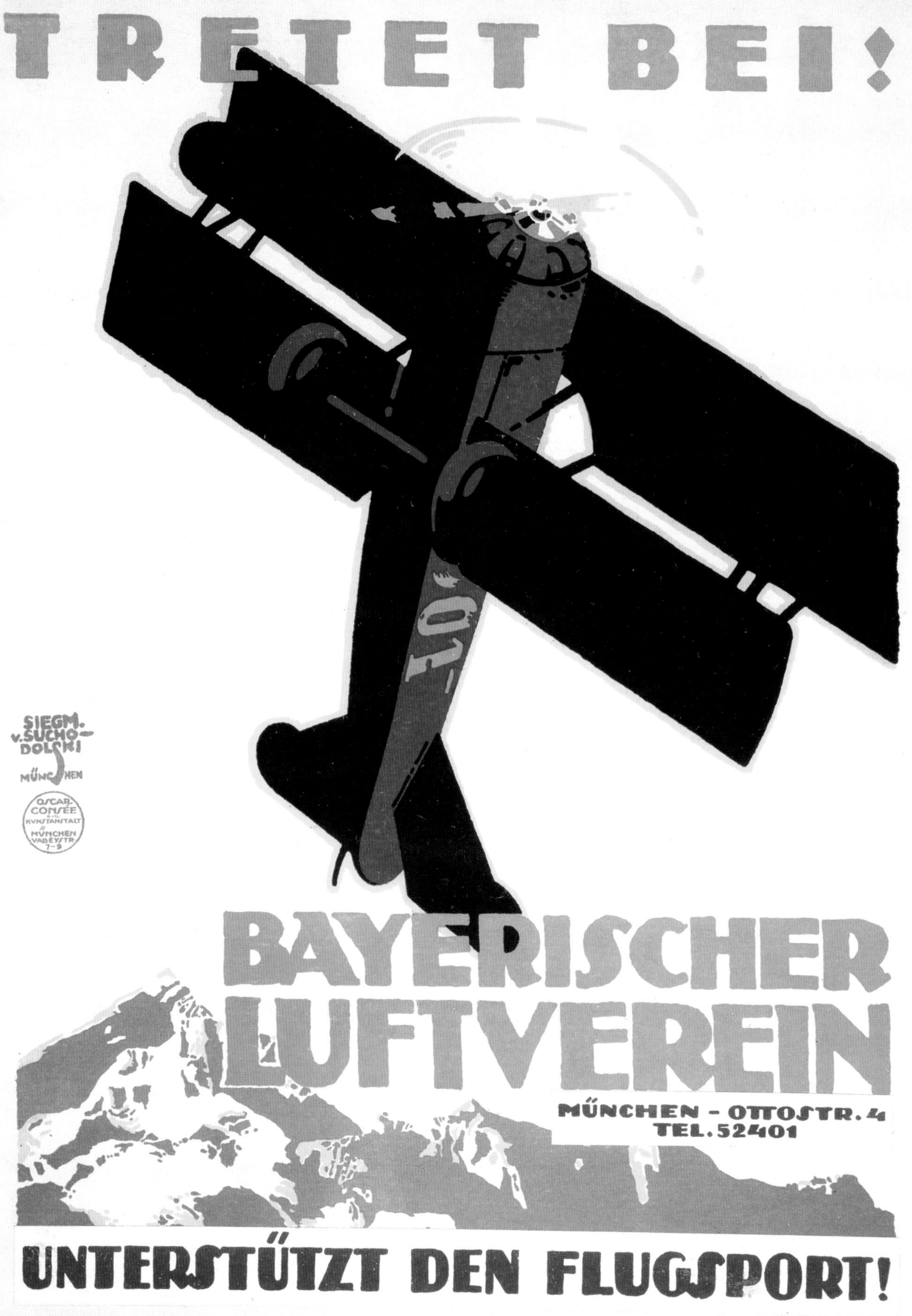

TRETET BEI!

BAYERISCHER LUFTVEREIN

MÜNCHEN - OTTOSTR. 4
TEL. 52401

UNTERSTÜTZT DEN FLUGSPORT!

CHAPTER TWO

JOIN THE CLUB

1913–1932

Aviation was getting organized. After Wilbur Wright made his European debut in 1908, sportsmen who had pioneered the use of autos and started the world's first auto clubs in 1902 began taking an interest in flight. Aero clubs, such as the Bayerischer Luftverein (Bavarian Air Club) featured in the poster at left, popped up everywhere, inviting one and all to fly: "*Tretet Bei!*—Join!," the poster says. Cities hosted exhibitions and record-breaking contests, and pilots became celebrities.

Some nations established aeronautical regiments even before the start of World War I in 1914—the first war in which aircraft had a significant presence. In 1911 in the Italo-Turkish War, Italy used the airplane in Libya as a platform from which to launch primitive bombs. During WWI all major combatants gradually incorporated bombers, fighters, and reconnaissance airplanes into

TRETET BEI
CIRCA 1918
12 x 8 1/2 in.

their larger strategies. By the end of WWI in 1918 all combatants had established military air services. While aviation did not significantly affect the outcome of WWI, the war had illustrated the airplane's potential. This promise, with the surge in nationalistic movements after WWI, energized the growth of civil aviation.

The Treaty of Versailles, which ended World War I, limited German aviation: Signers hoped to contain that nation's militarism. Ratified in 1920, the treaty decreed that Germany must scrap military aircraft and engines; it also spelled out restrictions on Germany's future aircraft production. As a result, aircraft manufacturers established factories outside Germany.

In the world of aviation, any nation's advancements were quickly noted by all other nations. The U.S., Japan, France, Great Britain, the Netherlands, Germany, and Italy vied for superiority. The Sociedad Colombo-Alemana de Transportes Aéreos (SCADTA), a Colombian-based company subsidized by German and Austrian entrepreneurs expanding aviation outside Germany, played a role in the development of U.S. aviation. In the early 1920s SCADTA developed air service linking Colombia's capital, Bogotá, with its major port, Barranquilla. Then, Peter Paul von Bauer, SCADTA's managing director, looked north to expand—into U.S. air space. Von Bauer's attempt in 1925 and '26 to initiate regular flights to Florida alarmed U.S. officials in the War and Navy Departments. To stop the German-Austrian company's intrusion, they advocated extending U.S. airlines into Latin America. This led to the creation of New York, Rio & Buenos Aires Line, Inc., and Pan American Airways. SCADTA's encroachment, U.S. interest in markets south of the border, and aviator Charles Lindbergh's momentous transatlantic flight resulted in the establishment of international airmail routes by the U.S. In 1928 the Foreign Air Mail Act was passed. It allowed the government, which controlled access to the nation's airmail routes, to begin awarding contracts to private U.S. companies to fly international routes.

In 1927, pilot Charles Lindbergh made the first nonstop solo flight across the Atlantic Ocean in his plane, the Spirit of St. Louis. *He told his story in the popular memoir, "We".*

C. G. Grey, editor of a prestigious aviation journal, summed up the spirit of the era: "We may be approaching an age of universal peace, but nobody seems to be taking any chances about it."

WE
1927
14 x 11 in..

JOIN THE AIR SERVICE

While last among the European nations that claimed a colony in North Africa, Italy was the first to use airplanes in combat. In the Italo-Turkish War (1911–12), the Italians, hoping to wrest Libya from the Ottoman (or Turkish) Empire, executed the first air reconnaissance operation and the first aerial bombing in combat, and took the first aerial reconnaissance photographs. Italian pilots made these aerial missions with an air service comprising seven French and two German aircraft.

The airplane seemed the perfect vehicle for avoiding the usual obstacles—deserts, jungles, unnavigable rivers—that Europeans had confronted while exploring, trading, and finally colonizing Africa. No matter how fierce and regal, the bayonet-carrying *Bersagleri*—an Italian soldier in a feathered helmet, as in the poster at left—still had to navigate treacherous landscapes and face tribal armies carrying European-made guns as powerful as his own. The airplane enabled Italian forces to rise above it all—though, as the poster reveals, ground troops were still the staple. In spite of the apparent advantage of attacking from the air, military establishments were slow to incorporate airplanes into battle plans.

ITALO-TURKISH WAR
CIRCA 1911
27 1/4 x 19 1/2 in.

CIVIL AVIATION'S WORLD WAR I ROOTS

COMPARED TO RECRUITING FOR THE REGULAR ARMY AND NAVY, ENLISTING young men in the newly created U.S. military air services was simple. The U.S. did not become a combatant in World War I until 1917, three years after its start. From 1914 to 1917, newspapers, magazines, and novels had amply described the horrors of trench warfare—and glorified the air war. The activities of the Lafayette Flying Corps—a group of some 200 Americans who already flew with the French Army Air Service—played a special role in popularizing combat flying among Americans. When the U.S. entered the war, industry leaders reluctantly turned away from making automobiles and building roads to manufacturing airplanes. Young Americans, however, were eager to earn their wings, and they flocked to recruiting stations. Posters like the one at right inspired recruits to sign up.

The use of airplanes in the war jump-started the commercial aviation industry. The war provided experience for aircraft manufacturers like German Hugo Junkers, whose aircraft would form the backbone of Lufthansa's early fleet, and Frenchman Pierre Latécoère, who founded airline Aéropostale, which would contribute to the foundation for Air France. War-trained pilots became industry pioneers: American Eddie Rickenbacker took control of Eastern Airlines in 1937; Australians W. Hudson Fysh and Paul McGinness founded Qantas in 1919; and American Ralph O'Neill started New York, Rio & Buenos Aires Line, Inc., in South America in 1927.

AMERICAN EAGLE
1917
27 x 20 1/2 in.

JOIN THE
ARMY AIR SERVICE
BE AN AMERICAN EAGLE!
ULT YOUR LOCAL DRAFT BOARD. READ THE ILLUSTRATED
KLET AT ANY RECRUITING OFFICE OR WRITE TO THE CHIEF
AL OFFICER OF THE ARMY, WAS NGTON D. C.

TOUS VOYAGES AÉRIENS
JEAN CARLU
LONDRES CALAIS CHERBOURG LE HÂVRE PARIS BORDEAUX
LYON MARSEILLE NICE CANNES ALGER

OVER HILL, OVER DALE, OVER SEA

French printmaker Jean Carlu's poster at left conveys Compagnie Aérienne Française's (CAF) leadership in aerial photography and mapmaking. Carlu was known for using bright colors, simple lines, and geometric shapes to create subtle abstractions of the products advertised in his posters. For the CAF poster, Carlu seems to have taken the aerial camera as his inspiration. The white airplane resembles an aerial camera. Take a step backward and the tail of the airplane becomes the shutter opening the lens. It focuses on a view of the French post-World War I sphere of influence, represented by the map below it.

CAF's greatest contribution to aviation history was producing aerial photographs for cartographers, industrialists, and city planners. CAF also launched one well-known pilot's career: Antoine de Saint-Exupéry, author of *The Little Prince* and other aviation-inspired books, flew for pioneering French airline Aéropostale. During the 1920s and '30s, a number of international celebrities, like Saint-Exupéry, came from the realm of aviation. Record-breaker Charles Lindbergh won fame when he crossed the North Atlantic solo in 1927; airline builders like Hugo Junkers in Germany and Pierre Latécoère in France drew attention when they expanded airline routes to South America and Africa.

CAF
1919
38 5/8 x 29 1/4 in.

RAIL-AIR-SERVICE

to SOUTH AMERICA

FROM YOUR HOME CITY
TO HAVANA · WEST INDIES
RIO DE JANEIRO · BUENOS
AIRES · SANTIAGO (CHILE)

"NYRBA"—A NEW SYMBOL IN AMERICAN TRANSPORTATION

Predominant business institutions in both the United States and South America have taken active part in the formation of the New York, Rio & Buenos Aires Line Inc., and in the establishment of its domestic and foreign policies. After two years of pioneering the company has in operation the longest single air line in the world on a 10,000 mile system spanning 16 countries and colonies of the Americas. Popularly known as the "Nyrba Air Lines," the project has been developed, not only to expedite business, but to increase the friendliness and cordiality between the peoples of the Western Hemisphere.

PENNSYLVANIA RAILROAD

The vast network of the Pennsylvania Railroad, and the great trunk lines and feeders of the Seaboard Airline Railway, Louisville & Nashville Railroad, and the Richmond, Fredericksburg & Potomac Railroad through the South, in conjunction with the Nyrba Airlines, provide direct de luxe, passenger and express service to and from North America, the West Indies and South America through train-to-plane transfer at Miami—from which Nyrba's great seagoing airliners speed Southward—supplying the only air passenger service between North America and Brazil, Argentina, Uruguay and Santiago, Chile. Homebound service is rendered in the same manner. From Seaboard trains passengers board Nyrba airliners, reaching Havana in two and a quarter hours, Rio de Janeiro in 7 days, Buenos Aires in 8 days. Fast planes from Buenos Aires fly to Santiago, Chile, in 8 hours—as against 41 hours by surface transportation. At Santiago airline connections are made for cities North and South in Chile, and at Yacuiba, for principal cities in Bolivia.

T. A. T.—MADDUX AIR LINES

The Transcontinental Air Transport—Maddux Air Lines, in conjunction with the Pennsylvania Railroad and the Santa Fe, provides 48-hour Los Angeles-New York rail-air service—covering the Southern route to Kansas City, St. Louis, Indianapolis, Columbus, and intermediate points . . . making direct connection with trains from these and many other cities to the Nyrba Air Lines at Miami.

EXPEDITING BUSINESS IN A BILLION DOLLAR MARKET

Nyrba passenger and express service, for the first time in history, brings the most distant capital of South America as near to us as Florida is to Oregon by rail. Exporters' representatives, traveling via Nyrba Lines, can now cover the entire East Coast Route (which has 72% of the wealth and 65% of the population of Latin America), in 75 days, with 50 days residence, as compared to 234 days required by the exigencies of surface travel. In addition, Nyrba's local representatives, and their staffs, are at the service of such representatives. Acting upon advance advices, Nyrba's local managers will secure accommodations, arrange appointments, provide in many ways for closer contacts and expedition in the transaction of business. This too, at a great saving of effort, tedious travel time and expense. This removal of the trade barriers of time and distance is of equal importance in the matter of air-express shipments of samples, spare parts, and such articles as are commonly shipped by railway express at home.

WORLD'S FINEST AIR EQUIPMENT

Nyrba's $2,500,000 fleet of high-powered, multi-motored, speedy air transports includes four types of planes. The major fleet consists of huge, 22-passenger Commodore airliners—fourteen of which are for use on the through route to Buenos Aires. These luxuriously fitted flying boats are pictured and described in the column to the left. The auxiliary fleet for fast mail, express and passenger service to intermediate and tributary points is illustrated and described at the right. It includes nine Sikorsky Amphibians; eight fast mail Fleetster planes, and four tri-motored Ford transports. Connecting service is maintained between the auxiliary fleet and the airliners at principal points on the through route. Speed, luxury and convenience are the predominating features of the entire fleet, providing the utmost in modern transportation.

AIR MAIL EXPEDITES BUSINESS

Nyrba's international air route links with the domestic air mail network to deliver postal correspondence from the West Indies and South America to principal cities in the United States and Canada weeks faster than ever before. Letters require but six and one-half days from Buenos Aires to Miami . . . but five and one-half days from Rio de Janeiro . . . and overnight domestic air-mail service delivers mail into New York early the next morning.

AIRLINERS LEAVE MIAMI Every THURSDAY

Nyrba seagoing airliners leave the seaplane base, Dinner Key, Miami, every morning at 8:30, for Havana, and every Thursday for the West Indies, Rio de Janeiro, Buenos Aires and intermediate points on the East Coast of South America. Flying low, "always over a landing field," the huge flying boats unquestionably provide the fastest and most luxurious way anywhere South.

FOR RATES AND FULL INFORMATION

Complete information regarding rates, baggage, railroad connections, and itinerary, may be had at any office of the airline, at the principal ticket offices of the Seaboard Airline Railway, T. A. T.-Maddux Air Lines, the Pennsylvania Railroad and associated railroads, and at select travel agencies and bureaus everywhere.

NYRBA'S PRINCIPAL FLEET

Fourteen Commodore flying boats, carrying 22 passengers and crew, have a range of 1,000 miles, and a cruising speed of 100 miles an hour. Each carries a crew of three—a pilot, assistant pilot, radio operator-steward. Equipped with two-way radio sets, pilots receive from Nyrba's network of ground stations weather bulletins at frequent intervals, from within a radius of 600 miles. Passenger accommodations are luxurious. Wide, clear-vision windows, broad, carpeted aisles, deep lounge seats, and a fully equipped dressing room contribute restful ease. Smoking is permitted; the cabins are roomier than a Pullman compartment, and as quiet as a railroad train. Commodore seagoing airliners are 68 feet overall, and have a wingspread of 100 feet.

NYRBA'S AUXILIARY FLEET

Each of the nine Sikorsky amphibian planes is built to carry 8 passengers and crew. They have a cruising speed of 105 miles an hour and a range of 600 miles.

The eight Fleetster fast mail planes have a capacity of 1750 pounds cargo, for either passengers, mail or express. They have a cruising speed of 158 miles an hour, a high speed of 187 miles an hour and a cruising range of 850 miles.

The four tri-motored Ford planes are equipped to carry 14 passengers and crew. They have a range of 600 miles at a speed of 100 miles an hour.

Pilots of all Nyrba planes are selected for their records and their experience. To qualify each must have had at least 2,000 hours in the air—equivalent to having flown a distance equal to nine times around the earth at the equator.

NEW YORK, RIO & BUENOS AIRES LINE INC.

IN WASHINGTON
PENNSYLVANIA RAILROAD, UNION STATION
613 14TH STREET, N. W.

IN NEW YORK
420 LEXINGTON AVENUE

IN WASHINGTON
SEABOARD AIRLINE RAILWAY
714 14TH STREET, N. W.

GOING INTERNATIONAL

AFTER SERVING WITH THE U.S. ARMY AIR SERVICE IN WORLD WAR I, FLYING ACE Ralph O'Neill continued his career, training pilots in Mexico and helping to establish civil and military aviation there. Working and traveling in Latin America, O'Neill began planning an airline to connect New York City with South America: In 1929 his New York, Rio & Buenos Aires Line, Inc. (NYRBA) was born. NYRBA's purpose, according to its first and only annual report, was "to establish an air transportation system linking the greatest nations of the new world, thereby promoting commerce and good will between these peoples."

In the late 1920s, NYRBA offered seaplane service from New York to Buenos Aires and intermediate points on the east coast of South America. NYRBA's fleet included Consolidated Commodore flying boats, Sikorsky amphibian planes, fast Fleetster mail planes, and Ford Tri-Motors. From 1929 to 1930, NYRBA flew U.S. mail from Buenos Aires to Santiago. The small airline was the only one, other than Pan American Airways (PAA), deemed reliable enough to be considered for a U.S. airmail contract. The poster at left drives home the idea that NYRBA was no fly-by-night operation. O'Neill was one of the first to believe that an airline could support itself by carrying passengers. With the onset of the Great Depression in 1930, however, the U.S. government forced NYRBA, in what O'Neill called "a shotgun wedding," to sell out to Pan American. This transaction consolidated Pan American's place as the nation's "chosen instrument" for international air transportation.

RAIL-AIR-SERVICE
1929
25 x 19 in.

"THALASSA"
MARSEILLE - AJACCIO - TUNIS
AIR UNION

THE FRENCH INITIATIVE

THE TREATY OF VERSAILLES FORCED GERMAN AVIATION INDUSTRIALISTS to establish much of their business abroad, but in France, airlines blossomed. Building on their WWI successes, the French government in 1920 created new departments to encourage aeronautical research, engineering, navigation, and weather reporting. Eager to display France's presence and progress worldwide, the government encouraged French airlines to carry not only mail but also passengers—across the English Channel to Britain, across the Mediterranean to North Africa, and later across the Atlantic to South America, and across the Alps to southern Europe and the Mideast. Lignes Aériennes Latécoère (founded in 1918) became the pioneering French aviation company Aéropostale in 1927; the important Compagnie Franco-Roumaine de Navigation Aérienne (1920) became CIDNA, Compagnie Internationale de Navigation Aérienne, in 1925. Other aviation leaders, Compagnie des Messageries Aériennes (1919) and Compagnie des Grands Express Aériens (1920), pooled resources to become Air Union in 1923.

Air Union flew the Paris-to-London route, and in 1926 began to fly to Ajaccio on the island of Corsica. In 1927 the airline offered service to Tunisia, a French protectorate. For elite travelers bored with standard cruises to Egypt, the Mediterranean, or the French Riviera, Air Union's four-passenger seaplanes transformed a tedious trip into a short—sometimes heart-stopping—flight. Known as the Thalassa (meaning "sea" in Greek) fleet, Air Union catered to these royal, wealthy, classically educated patrons.

THALASSA
CIRCA 1927
39 1/4 x 24 in.

ITALY'S NATIONAL CARRIER

IN 1934 ITALY'S PRIME MINISTER BENITO MUSSOLINI CONSOLIDATED THE nation's four airlines into one. He envisioned this national carrier as a modern-day Roman soldier might—as the vehicle with which he would regain the lands and glory of the Roman Empire. He named the line Ala Littoria, or "Winged Lictor." A *lictor* was a soldier in ancient Rome who carried a bundle of reeds overlaid with an axe to prove his rank and might. Ala Littoria's logo, at the bottom left of the poster, was the black silhouette of a swallow superimposed over the bundle, or *fasces*. From this term the political movement Fascism drew its name. Clearly, Mussolini pinned great hopes on the airline.

In Italy, as in other European nations in this period between the two World Wars, lines between civil and military aviation sometimes blurred. In 1933 Mussolini directed Italy's air minister, Italo Balbo, to organize and lead a squadron of 25 flying boats across the Atlantic to the U.S. Balbo returned a hero, and Mussolini made him head of the Italian Air Force. At the same time, Mussolini ordered aircraft designers to build airplanes bigger than the flying boats—ones that could be used as bombers in wartime. By 1935 Ala Littoria was flying the tri-motor Savoia-Marchetti SM75 pictured at right. While some Ala Littoria craft were flying regular European routes, others were in a campaign to add Abyssinia (now Ethiopia) to Italy's colonial holdings. By 1936 Italy controlled a large portion of East Africa (Abyssinia, Eritrea, and Italian Somaliland) and Ala Littoria was flying there regularly.

ALA LITTORIA
1935
40 x 28 in.

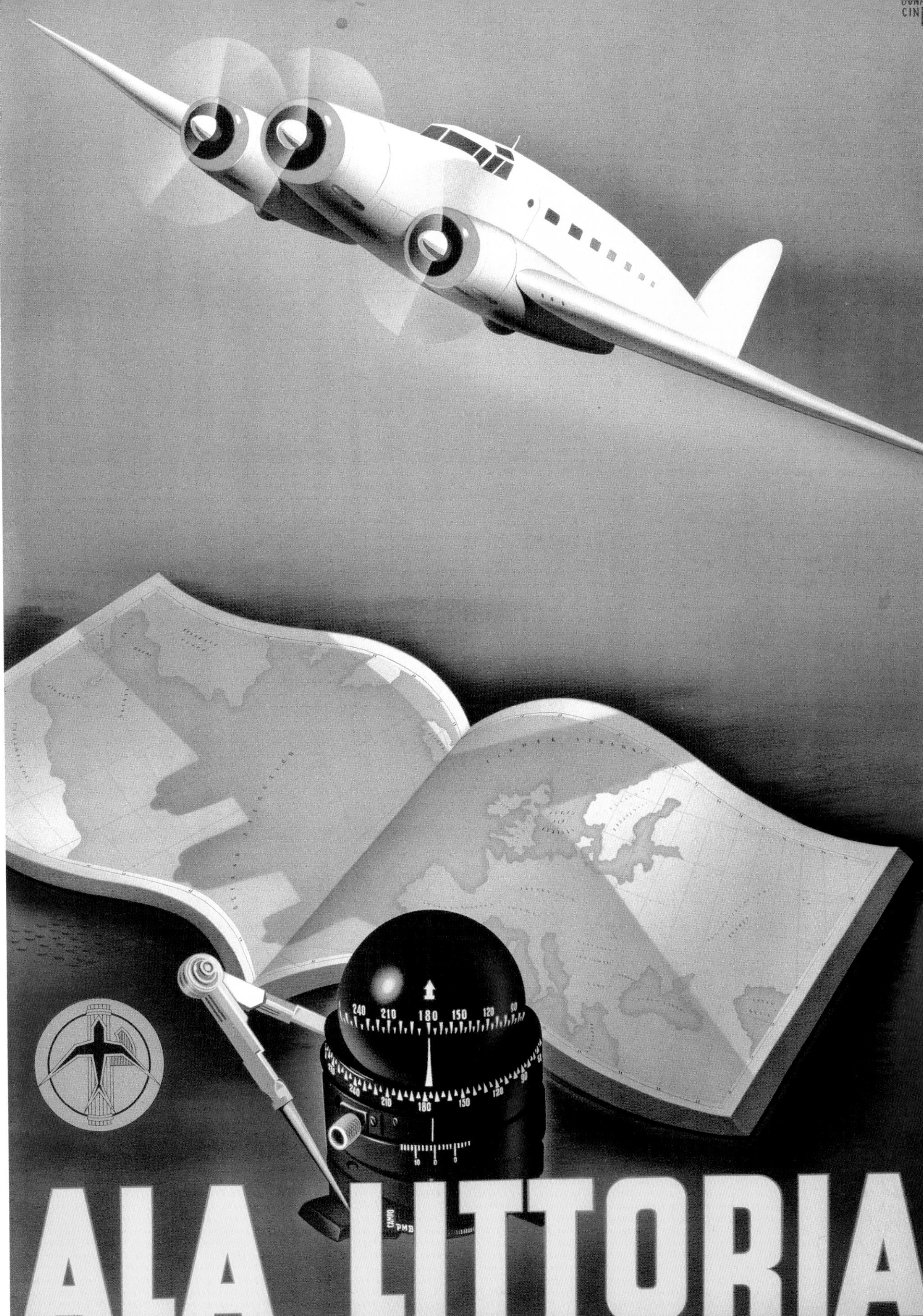
ALA LITTORIA

THE IMPERIAL WAY

WORLD WAR I LEFT GREAT BRITAIN WITH A SURPLUS OF TRAINED PILOTS, mechanics, and aircraft, and with airfields from London to Cairo. Britain was ready to build airlines. However, Secretary of State for Air Winston Churchill refused to grant government subsidies to build the commercial airline industry. Aviation entrepreneurs were dismayed, but they persevered: Privately funded airlines began crossing the English Channel to service points north. Their perseverance paid off. In 1924 the British government consolidated existing airlines to create a national carrier, suitably named Imperial Airways.

By 1931 it took only six days to get to India. Though not exactly direct, the routes significantly cut the usual travel time by train and ship: Passengers flew from London to Paris in a 38-seat Handley-Page H.P. 42s, then boarded a train for Brindisi, Italy, where they took a 12-seat Short S.8 Calcutta seaplane across the Mediterranean to Athens, and then flew to Haifa, before continuing to India. Imperial resorted to this convoluted arrangement to avoid negotiating with Italian Prime Minister Mussolini for landing rights in Italy. In 1931 Imperial flew 7-seat de Havilland Hercules planes through Persia (now Iran) to Karachi (now in Pakistan) landing along the Persian Gulf. In 1932 Persia canceled Imperial's landing rights; so Imperial sent flights through northern Arabia (now Kuwait and the states of the Persian Gulf). When in 1934 the British government announced the Empire Airmail Scheme—an ambitious plan to link Britain with her colonies by air—Imperial began to grow at an unprecedented rate.

6 DAYS
1931
30 x 20 in.

USE AIRMAIL

Airmail played a major role in reestablishing diplomatic, economic, and emotional ties among Europeans after World War I. As aircraft became faster and more efficient, airlines added cities each year to the continental airmail route system, speeding letters and packages to their destinations. Airmail, promoted in the poster at left, also accelerated Europeans' adjustments to a postwar map of redrawn national boundaries, with new nations carved mainly from the former Austro-Hungarian Empire.

At first, airplanes were not powerful enough to make a profit carrying passengers; they relied on carrying the mail to stay in business. Airmail paved the way for air transportation. Before 1918 airline routes did not exist. During the 1920s and early '30s, airlines gave pilots the task of scouting air routes to later carry passengers across Europe, to South America, and across the North Atlantic to the U.S. In the U.S., federal money paid for building a network of beacons, which pilots used to navigate across the mountains and featureless prairies of the continent. In Europe, pilots followed coastlines, river valleys, and railroads. The British even dug a 310-mile trench across the deserts of Jordan and western Iraq to help Imperial Airways pilots navigate from Cairo to Baghdad, first with mail, then passengers.

AIR MAIL
CIRCA 1932
20 1/8 x 15 1/8 in

EUROPA-UNION
Junkers
LUFT-POST-
FRACHT-VERKEHR
GENF-MÜNCHEN-BUDAPEST ◆ MÜNCHEN-FRANKFURT A/M.
BERLIN-STOCKHOLM-HELSINGFORS-RIGA-BERLIN ◆ STOCKHOLM-ZÜRICH IN 18 STUNDEN.

THE UBIQUITOUS F-13

1.

Between 1921 and 1926 aircraft designer and entrepreneur Hugo Junkers traveled the European continent, seeking airmail and airline companies needing aircraft. Finding markets in Finland, Estonia, Latvia, the Free City of Danzig, Austria, Hungary, and Switzerland, he built a broad network of clients. Junkers's all-metal airplane, the F-13, with its distinctive corrugated metal skin, became a common sight on airstrips all over Europe. The first all-metal, commercial plane, the F-13 served as mail carrier and passenger transport. It also became the flagship for Junkers's own airline, Europa-Union (1), founded in 1925 and featured in the poster at left. In later versions, the cockpit was enclosed. The oval window at the front (2) gave pilots a view of the ground for navigational purposes. Designed for four passengers, the F-13 could carry substantial loads of airmail and cargo.

2.

Artist T. Dornhecker's poster, with bold images and wording, captures Junkers's blind optimism about the future of Europa-Union and German aviation. Porters stream to the plane's open door, the focal point of the poster (3). In 1926 the German government subsumed Junkers's Europa-Union Airline into the newly created national airline, Deutsche Lufthansa.

3.

EUROPA-UNION
CIRCA 1925
10 x 7 in.

AIR MAIL

reaches every city

REACHING OUT TO AMERICA

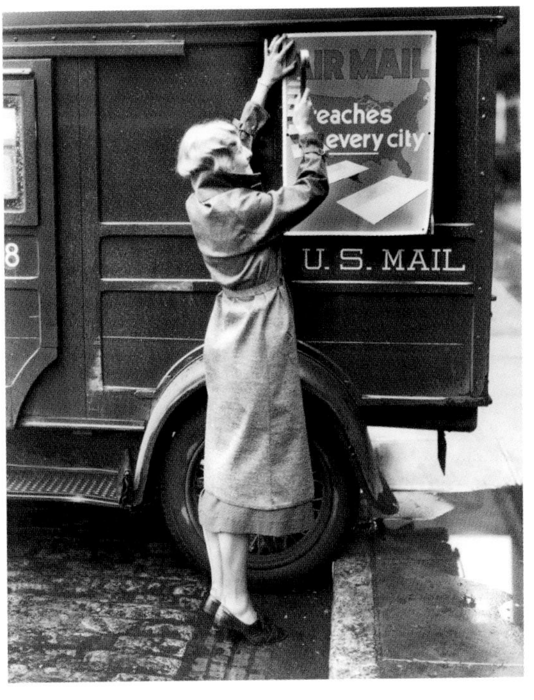

In 1932, 10,000 posters like this one, promoting airmail, were displayed on mail trucks and in post office lobbies.

ANNOUNCE! INFORM! CONVERT! Throughout the late 1920s and early '30s, posters played a significant role in convincing Americans of the need to speed up the delivery of their letters and general correspondence. Unlike businessmen, bankers, and lawyers who were quick to see airmail's potential, ordinary letter writers could not justify spending a few extra cents just for better service. An onslaught of advertising changed their minds. Slogans like "Use Airmail" appeared on city sidewalks, mail chutes, and posters decorating U.S. Post Office trucks and neighborhood post offices alike. This often-repeated message reminded citizens that the airmail network reached beyond rural mailboxes and connected small-town Americans to the nation's urban centers. In 1932 post office representatives traveled the country to raise awareness for airmail service. In El Paso, Texas—self-proclaimed "International Air Center of the West"—a display in post office windows during the city's first Air Week featured the poster at left, its bright style the epitome of 1930s public service announcements.

AIR MAIL REACHES
1932
40 x 32 in..

FRANCE-SYRIE-INDOCHINE
CHINE DU SUD - INDES NÉERLANDAISES
ITALIE - GRÈCE - IRAQ - PERSE - INDE - SIAM
A. M. CASSANDRE
PAR AVION
VIA
AIR-ORIENT
POSTE AÉRIENNE
GAGNEZ DU TEMPS:
TOUT VOTRE COURRIER PAR AVION
1932 ALLIANCE GRAPHIQUE LOUPOT-CASSANDRE PARIS. 34, RUE MARC-SEGUIN XVIIIe

CONNECTING TO THE COLONIES

ON FRENCH AIRLINE AIR-ORIENT, MAIL FROM THE FAR EAST ARRIVED IN France in record time. Between 1929 and 1931, Air-Orient cut travel time between Paris and Saigon, paring down mail service from ten to eight days. Designer A. M. Cassandre's poster at left celebrates the achievement—juxtaposing Saigon (then in Indochina) and Paris as if they were next-door neighbors. An airbrushed sky, silhouetted airplane, and gauzy letter-carrying dove link the distant capitals. The image encourages French citizens to rethink their relationship to Indochina (now Vietnam, Laos, and Cambodia), one of France's farthest-flung colonies.

The pastel image belies the arduous nature of the trip. The flight was long and punctuated with stops. As an Air-Orient timetable explained, "Planes may also land at intermediary stations other than the principal ones. There is no guarantee that the daily stages will be adhered to strictly." Lioré et Olivier LO242 seaplanes flew people and post from Marseilles, France, to Beirut, Lebanon. From Beirut, car service delivered travelers and mail to Damascus, Syria, where they boarded Breguet 280 airplanes to Baghdad, Iraq. Bureaucrats, businessmen, and sightseers deplaned there, finding other means to reach their destinations. Then Air-Orient's airplanes—loaded only with mail and diplomatic pouches—headed east to Saigon. In 1933, Air-Orient, Air Union, CIDNA (Compagnie Internationale de Navigation Aérienne), Société Générale de Transport Aérien, and Aéropostale joined to create France's national flag carrier, Air France.

AIR-ORIENT
1932
31 5/8 x 23 5/8 in.

AIRPLANES AND PROPAGANDA

It looks as if the airplane just flew into this 1930s-era poster. Take away the airplane—a Fokker F.XI—and the scene seems to predate the poster by at least 30 years. The docked ships, at the poster's bottom left, are old technology, and the women wear traditional Korean dress. The gray, pale pink, and red shades of their clothing indicate that they belong to the working class and are dressed for a celebration, perhaps the inauguration of the Shinkyo-Ranan route, which Manchuria Air Transport, Ltd. opened in 1932. Since 1931 Japan had occupied Manchuria—a large region of northeastern China and part of Korea. The Shinkyo route worked this way: Ships from Japan brought mail to Ranan (now Ranam, North Korea); then airplanes transported the mail to the Manchurian city of Shinkyo (now Changchun, in northeast China).

The poster, announcing mail service, plays a propaganda role. The women look pleased, in spite of the changes brought about by the 1931 Japanese occupation. One woman (with her hair in a bun, indicating she is married) holds a letter to her heart—perhaps from her husband sent to Manchuria's interior to help build new cities. The other woman, with a pigtail (a style worn by unmarried women) and balancing a pot, suggests the traditional past. Juxtaposing old and new, the poster implies that technology will bring progress and harmony to Japan and its colonies.

MANCHURIA AIR TRANSPORT
1930s
40 1/2 x 28 1/8 in.

滿洲航空株式會社
新京—羅南線開始

ZUGSPITZE
1925
23 1/2 x 27 1/2 in.

YOUR AERO CLUB

The scene in this 1925 poster at first seems serene and idyllic—pastel tones, the skier gazing at an airplane gliding over the Zugspitze, Germany's highest mountain. At second glance, however, the poster also conveys an aura of anticipation and energy. The skier balances on the edge of the precipice, elbows up, skis at the ready, as if waiting to see what heights he and the pilot might conquer next.

The monoplane, an Udet UX, is named for World War I German flying ace Ernst Udet, who lent his name to the aircraft company Udet-Flugzeugbau—privately funded by an American—in 1921. For the next four years, he flew the company's racers and stunt aircraft in exhibitions, to great acclaim. On January 31, 1925, Udet raced 13 other pilots from Schleissheim airfield near Munich to Garmisch-Partenkirchen near the Austrian border. According to a newspaper account, the race was a "perfect start" to the 1925 flying season, and the exhibition was a "perfect example" of the absurdity of post-WWI restrictions on German aviation. The poster's Udet UX and the skier's bib display the number "4." Such solidarity between the two sports hints at the nationalistic fervor of sport exhibitions in the 1920s and '30s.

II SA ON DE AERONAVTICA
EXPOSICION IBERO-AMERICANA
PARRILLA
XXVIII SEVILLA
SEVILLA 1929
REAL AERO CLVB
DE
ANDALVCIA

CLUB SPIRIT: EXPOS AND EXHIBITIONS

ORGANIZED AERONAUTICAL ACTIVITIES PROLIFERATED DURING THE years between the wars. In 1929 alone, the United States, Belgium, England, and Spain hosted international aeronautical exhibitions. Almost every nation in South America and Europe claimed at least one active aero club. Although the clubs operated in the best spirit of civil aviation, a strong militaristic undertone pervaded all their activities.

The bright red galleon in the poster at left reminds participants and fair visitors to the 1929 Ibero-American Exposition in Seville, Spain, that Spain boasted a long tradition of exploration, technological leadership, and colonial success. Compared to 20th-century Germany and France, however, Spain's aeronautical industry lagged. Three Spanish pilots, including Roman Franco, brother of Francisco Franco (Fascist leader of Spain from 1936 until 1973), flew the first direct flight from Europe to South America in 1926. The flight, though record-breaking, did not stimulate airline building in Spain. In contrast, France, Germany, Italy, and the Netherlands, with the help of the military, private entrepreneurs, and aero clubs, had parlayed their aeronautical experience into creating postal routes and airlines. By the time of the Ibero-American Exposition in 1929, France, via airline Aéropostale, was making regular flights from Europe to South America, through Spanish-controlled lands. And Germany was not far behind. In 1929 German aircraft began flying through Seville, Spain, on their way to Brazil.

ANDALUCIA
1929
35 1/4 x 25 1/4 in.

FLY THERE
G-EBVG
EUROPE - EGYPT - INDIA
IMPERIAL AIRWAYS
THE MODERN WAY

CHAPTER THREE

FLY THERE!

1927–1939

By the 1920s, airline posters featured the dynamic and direct interactions taking place between people and technology. Posters hawking the wares of the newly created airline industry urged bureaucrats, diplomats, industrialists, colonialists, and travelers to pack their bags, board a plane, and see the world anew.

The era's posters, like the one at left, touted particular aircraft, bearing recognizable registration numbers and monikers. They showed cross sections of airplanes, listed timetables, and built cachet for airline routes named in the same romantic spirit that railroad companies named trains such as France's luxury Golden Arrow or the U.S.'s transcontinental Sunset Limited. Flying was such a novel experience that posters highlighting basic details—the number of engines or seating arrangements—were enticing. These "plane facts" suggested that the consumer's experience, from boarding to deplaning, regardless of the destination, was itself worth the price of the ticket.

FLY THERE
1928
40 x 25 in.

Airlines came of age at a seemingly inauspicious time. The political and physical fallout of World War I had drastically depressed the economies of most European nations. In the United States, the stock market crash of 1929 sent the U.S. economy into a tailspin that lasted until the end of the 1930s—known as the Great Depression. Then, once again, nations around the globe became entangled in another devastating world war. Yet in spite of the economic troubles worldwide, the airline industry grew. Running an airline—especially a national flag carrier—not only gave a nation status but also stimulated its aviation industry. By 1934, the governments of Europe's largest nations, including Great Britain, France, Italy, and Germany, as well as its smallest, like Hungary, all had created subsidized national carriers. Hungary had been formed in the reapportionment of the Austro-Hungarian Empire, dissolved by the treaties ending World War I. Its newly founded airline was Magyar Légiforgalmi Részvénytársasá (Hungarian Air-traffic Co. Ltd.). Known as Malert, the airline flew Dutch- and Italian-made aircraft from Budapest to Vienna, once a day in each direction. Malert shared the skies with KLM, Air France, Deutsche Lufthansa, Imperial Airways, and Ala Littoria.

Advertisers did not hesitate to play on the public's naive expectations for the thrilling new aeronautical technology. In airline advertising materials, including posters, artists freely interpreted aviation's accomplishments and ballyhooed its power and promise. In the poster at right, for instance, the airplane is as detailed as a photograph, while the train below it is cartoonlike. Some posters made much of the fact that flying afforded passengers an extraordinary, almost godlike, view of Earth. Some airline posters appealed to potential consumers' fantasies about the transformative power of flying. These posters implied that taking to the air in one of these magic machines could turn a person into a modern entrepreneur or, even more fantastically, a technologically empowered pioneer and leader of the 20th century. Air travel, so the posters suggested, not only transported passengers high above people's amazed and admiring gazes—as shown in the Imperial Airways poster on page 84—but also compressed time and space with quick flights across routes that once seemed endless.

Eight airlines—in addition to Austria's Österreichische Luftverkehrs A.G. (OLAG) featured here—provided domestic service to Vienna, "the turntable for international air traffic." But it was railroad service, not these other airlines, that was OLAG's true competition in 1931.

HEUTE....FLIEGT MAN
1938
19 3/4 x 12 1/2 in.

FLY TO WINTER SPORT
Switzerland in 3 flying hours
IMPERIAL AIRWAYS & SWISSAIR

THE PROPELLER SET

As soldiers returned home to their families after World War I, society's upper classes left home. Traveling by train, cruise ship, and increasingly by airplane, debutantes, diplomats, businessmen, and others who could afford the time and tickets flocked to seaside and mountain resorts. Newspapers and magazines reported the whereabouts of these globe-trotters, noting which hotels, resorts, and destinations were the most popular. When middle-class tourists encroached on these bastions of privilege, elites built summer homes in restricted "colonies" and sought more remote places to visit. They used planes to speed their travel, guard their privacy, and maintain the geography of leisure to which they were accustomed.

In 1938, Imperial Airways, with Swissair, offered direct flights to Zurich, illustrated at left. This poster touts "3 flying hours," but neglects to mention the hours travelers had to spend on trains, after deplaning, to reach Swiss ski resorts. Upon touching down in Zurich, passengers traveled two to three hours by train to Davos, St. Moritz, or Grindelwald. Still, British skiers patronized Imperial's new de Havilland service (using D.H. 91 Albatross airplanes). Flying cut back overall travel time, effectively bringing winter sport a little closer.

FLY TO WINTER SPORT
1938
19 3/4 x 12 1/2 in.

FLY
AMERICAN

MAIL • PASSENGERS • EXPRESS

New York to Boston

Fast Frequent Schedules

$13.90 One Way

Reduction on Round Trips

AMERICAN AIRWAYS

COAST to COAST – CANADA – MEXICO

SELLING TO THE BUSINESS WORLD

In the 1930s, airline agents attempted to sell tickets to travelers by barraging passersby with placards like these in the American Airways ticket office window in Jackson, Mississippi.

IN SPITE OF THE DIRE ECONOMIC environment following the stock market crash in 1929, the U.S. airline industry continued to open new routes, build more airplanes, and design new models. By 1933 an upswing in express mail and passenger traffic was offsetting the downturn in regular mail. While many letter writers decided that paying for airmail delivery was not worth the shorter delivery time, businessmen with deadlines were willing to pay higher prices for express delivery or to fly to a meeting if that meant, as an American Airways timetable put it, cutting travel time by "more than half."

The Aircraft Year Book for 1934 attributed the remarkable increase in commercial air services to airlines making service so attractive "it was becoming indispensable." Companies relied on newspaper and journal ads, along with posters, billboards, and store placards to win customers. American's ticket offices nationwide featured the placard at left. The airline judged that convenient schedules, night flights, and faster planes, like the Stinson SM 6000 pictured through the window, would continue to increase passenger miles.

FLY AMERICAN
1933
17 x 13 in.

canada and adirondacks
thousand islands
murray bay
MARINE AIR TRANSPORT COMPANY
northern lakes
pocono mountains
lake mohawk
cape cod
long island
shore resorts
florida
METROPOLITAN SEAPLANE TERMINAL
PIER B EXCHANGE PLACE JERSEY CITY
call montgomery 5·3660

SOCIETY FLIES

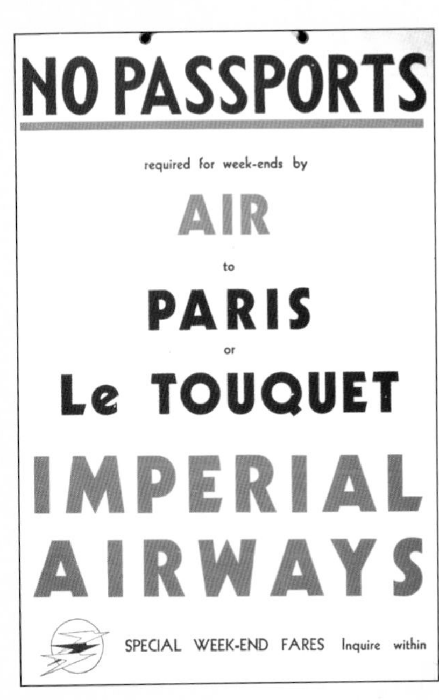

1.

After World War I, travel across international borders in Europe became increasingly difficult. By 1926, passport rules had become so strict that they were impeding postwar reconstruction. Hotel and casino owners argued for returning to the more lenient prewar passport regulations. But whatever the regulations, the wealthy were not staying home. Le Touquet, the "most lighthearted of the nearer French watering places," according to an Imperial Airways's 1932 timetable, catered to the rich, famous, and royal. Situated on France's northern coast, Le Touquet was "one flying hour" from London; even better, the resort town did not require British, Belgian, or French passengers to present passports for short visits (1).

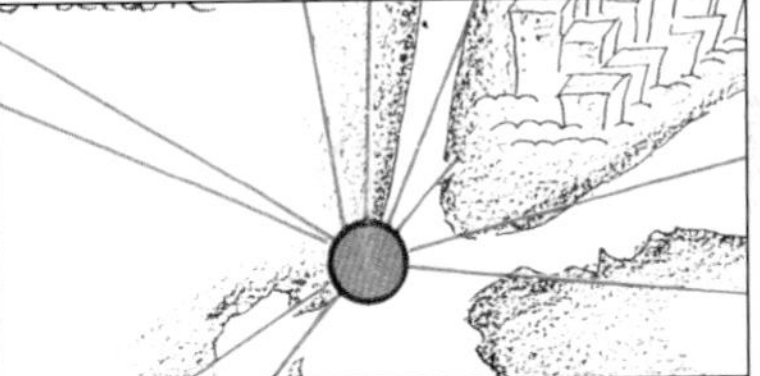

2.

U.S. vacationers moved freely between the states and into Canada. Automobiles allowed many to visit places once accessible only to the wealthy. In turn, airplanes allowed the wealthy to access even more exclusive spots. New York commuters flew Marine-Air Transport (MAT), at left, from New York City to second homes in Lake Mohawk, New Jersey (2), and in Murray Bay, Canada (3), where Pres. William Howard Taft's family summered.

3.

MARINE-AIR TRANSPORT; NO PASSPORTS
1932; 1932
17 x 11 in.; 12 1/2 x 8 1/2 in.

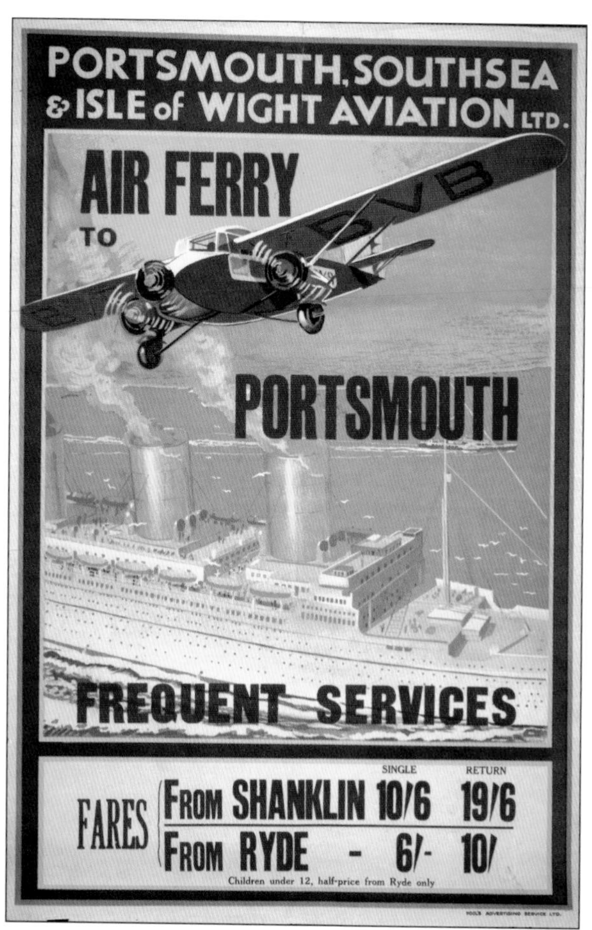

AIR SERVICE FOR THE SUMMER CROWD

When railroad service connected London to Southampton and Portsmouth in the 1840s, high society, writers, scientists, and royalty began visiting the Isle of Wight. Alighting from trains, they crossed The Solent channel by ferry to their manor houses. In 1932, Portsmouth, Southsea & Isle of Wight Aviation Company (PSIOWA) above, introduced an "air ferry." Frequent and fast—only a few minutes—PSIOWA's flights carried travelers from Portsmouth to the isle every summer until WWII.

AIR FERRY TO PORTSMOUTH
1932
30 x 20 in.

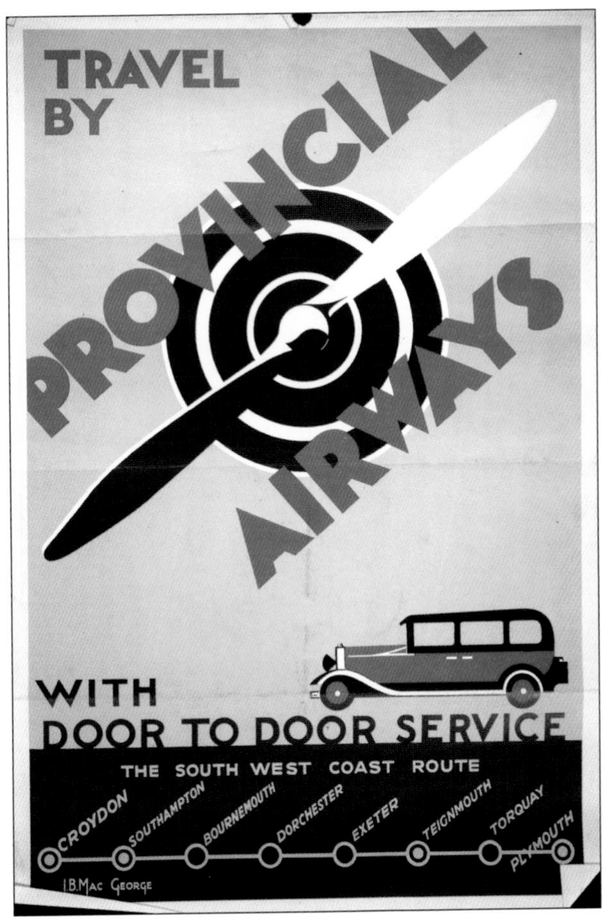

Like PSIOWA, Provincial Airways, above, was a small, privately owned airline. In 1934 Provincial offered service between Plymouth and London's Croydon Airport with stops at Southampton and Teignmouth. The service combined airplanes and cars to speed day-trippers and vacationers to their destinations—faster than any train. In 1935 the Great Western Railway's *Cornish Riviera Express* carried passengers one way from London to Penzance in 6 hours and 30 minutes. Two Provincial passengers made a *round-trip* between the same points, with time for lunch, in just 6 hours and 10 minutes.

PROVINCIAL
1934
30 x 20 in.

The Empire's Air Line

ENGLAND - ITALY - EGYPT - INDIA

IMPERIAL AIRWAYS

IA/X/20 5m 1929/4

H.E.WATSON.

Posters in Stockholm's Bromma Airport in 1936 advertise Swedish, Finnish, French,and British airlines serving the Swedish capital.

FLYING THE FRENCH FLAG

CREATING NATIONAL AIR CARRIERS WAS A SIGNIFICANT STEP IN THE GROWTH of European airlines after World War I. Air France celebrated its founding with posters that jubilantly expressed the nation's hopes for aviation. Airline mergers were nothing new. By the late 1920s, a score of French airlines served France's domestic and colonial markets. A few years later, only four remained; in 1933 the French government consolidated these survivors into France's first national carrier, Air France. In the poster at left, an Air France pilot holds high what looks like a puzzle piece in the shape of France plucked from a jigsaw puzzle of the world. Behind him, the dark, stylized shadow of the white airplane embraces the globe. The poster seems nonthreatening; yet it suggests the airplane's role as an instrument of domestic defense and national prestige.

AIR FRANCE
1933
39 1/2 x 27 1/2 in.

Fly
through
Europe
by
IMPERIAL
AIRWAYS

FLY: BE MODERN

How did the airline industry convince the world that the airplane was the quintessential expression of the modern era? Sometimes posters depicted an airplane subsumed into a sleek, abstract image of speed and motion. Others posters, such as the one at left, employed caricature: Artist Paul Scheurich created the jolly, overadorned naval commander marveling at Imperial Airways's Handley Page H.P. 42.

Scheurich's jolly gentleman had plenty of company among the characters of airline posters and publicity. One Lufthansa poster showed a cartoon image of a beribboned and bonneted gentlewoman precariously leaning out the window of her carriage to take a look at the Junkers all-metal, tri-motor airplane flying above her. French artist Georges Villa, working for France's Air Ministry, resurrected Joseph Prudhomme, a 19th-century French caricature of the smug, self-satisfied middle-class citizen. Villa showed Prudhomme advising a 20th-century version of himself against the folly of clinging to the status quo: Prudhomme leans over the shoulder of the 20th-century man who dismissively views an airplane flying above him. Declares Prudhomme with a nudge: "I didn't believe in the railroad either."

IMPERIAL AIRWAYS
1931
40 x 25 in.

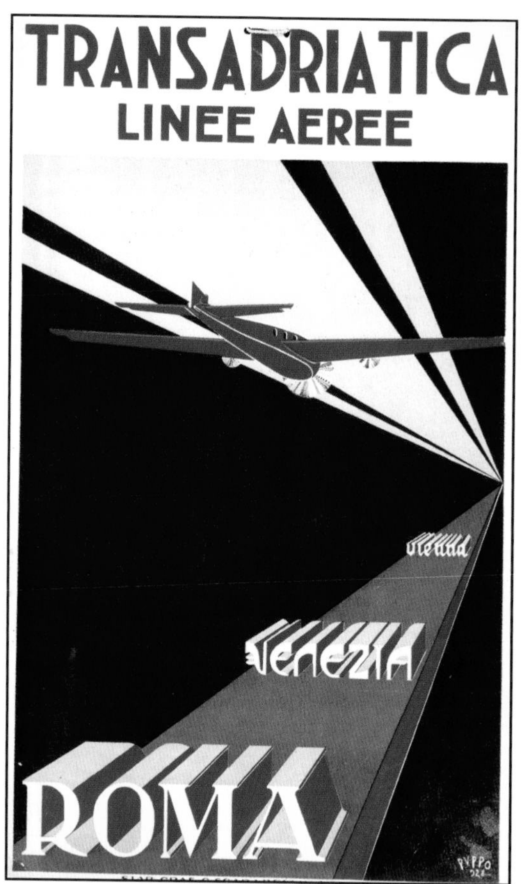

FLYING INTO THE FUTURE

IN 1929 ARTIST MARIO PUPPO CREATED A STREAMLINED LOOK IN HIS POSTER, above, for the Italian airline Transadriatica. Using distinctive fonts for each city along Transadriatica's newest route, Puppo featured the city names in a sleek design. A band of green, representing terra firma, connects Rome, Venice, and Vienna. Above the airplane, lines of force dive into the distance, enhancing the poster's dynamic feel and suggesting that the airplane's speed

TRANSADRIATICA
1933
19 1/2 x 11 3/4 in.

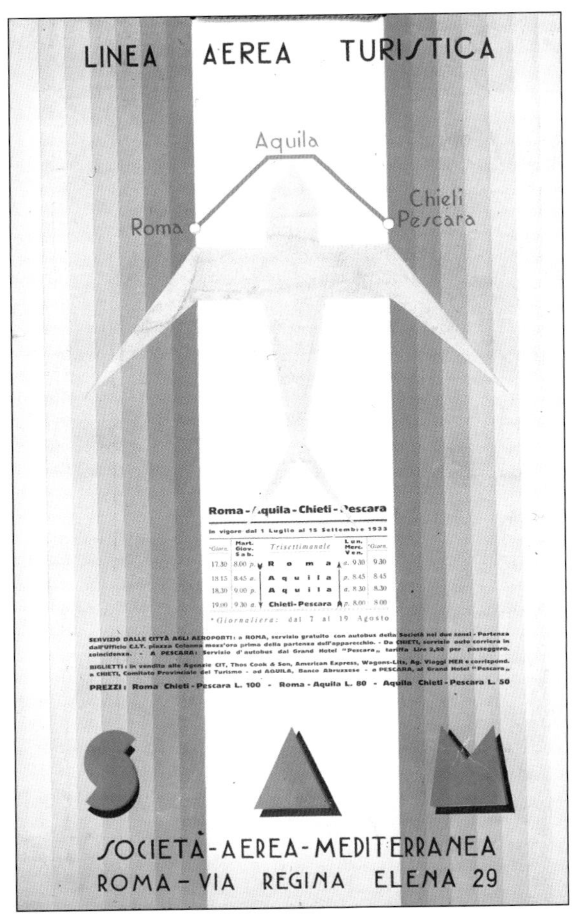

is far greater than that of the Junkers-G 24's 113-mile-an-hour limit. The plane flies toward the horizon, as if urging viewers to take a flight to the world of the future. In the 1930s Italian airlines often used abstract designs in their advertising. In 1933 state-owned Società Aerea Mediterranea (SAM) took over Transadriatica's routes and created even more abstract graphics, as in the poster above. In 1934 Italy's Prime Minister Benito Mussolini created the national airline Ala Littoria, which, in turn, took over SAM.

SAM
1933
15 1/2 x 9 7/8 in.

AIRLINE OF THE RISING SUN

IN AUGUST 1931, ONE MONTH BEFORE JAPAN OCCUPIED MANCHURIA, A *NEW YORK Times* article called the Japanese aviation industry "backward." Even if Japan could not match its contemporaries in the United States and Europe, the Japanese had great interest in building both an air force and an airline industry. Perhaps in response to the criticism expressed in the *Times,* Japan Air Transport Co., Ltd. (JAT)—Japan's national carrier—commisioned Japanese artist Seiichi to create a poster showing Japan's international perspective to the world. The traditional Japanese *Bijin ga* or beauty picture, a convention that used a woman's face as the hook to advertise myriad unrelated products, may have inspired Seiichi's eclectic design mixing Eastern and Western styles. The poster's message revolves around the familiar image of a woman, though one dressed in Western rather than Japanese clothes. The woman's casual wave, instead of the *Bijin ga*'s direct stare, draws the eye into the poster, first to the Fokker Super Universal airplane flying above the tarmac and then down to the pilot gazing her way. The woman boarding the waiting Fokker F.VIIb-3m wears a kimono, but with a modern pattern. In the background, the rising sun—Japan's national symbol on its flag—makes the poster glow.

By the 1920s three private companies were delivering mail and passengers throughout Japan. In 1928 the Japanese government consolidated these pioneering companies into one government-subsidized Japan Air Transport Co., Ltd. (JAT). In 1931 Japan enlisted JAT's aircraft and pilots to annex Manchuria. Suddenly the image of the rising sun in the placid JAT poster takes on new meaning.

JAPAN AIR TRANSPORT CO., LTD.
CIRCA 1931
36 1/2 x 24 1/4 in.

JAPAN AIR TRANSPORT CO., LTD.

J-BBJO

SEIICHI

TOKIO 東京 OSAKA 大阪 FUKUOKA 福岡 URUSAN 蔚山 KEIJO 京城 HEIJO 平壌 DAIREN 大連

日本航空輸送株式會社

WILSON AIRWAYS

SPECIAL CHARTERS - REGULAR SERVICES

FLY: BE A COLONIALIST

"Even now, it seems almost unbelievable that I had my Monday morning breakfast in Singapore, and had my following Monday's lunch in Piccadilly, London," reported a businessman in the pages of the April 1936 issue of the *Imperial Airways Gazette*. By flying, the businessman cut weeks off the trip usually made by steamship liner.

Air travel sped mail, businessmen, and colonial government officers across the often roadless and unmapped expanses of British East Africa (now Kenya, Uganda, and Tanzania) and between Africa and Britain. On one of her many trips back home, Mrs. Florence Kerr Wilson, who was running her late husband's farm in Kenya, decided to start an airline to serve this market. In 1929 she founded Wilson Airways, which would cater to gold miners, coffee plantation owners, and other farmers within East Africa. By 1937 Wilson Airways, depicted at left, was chartering flights and flying small de Havilland D.H.84 Dragon airplanes on regularly scheduled flights timed to coordinate with Imperial Airways flying-boat service to and from East Africa's Lake Victoria. Wilson Airways made East Africa accessible to colonial entrepreneurs and also helped to develop commercial aviation in that part of the world.

WILSON
CIRCA 1937
19 3/4 x 12 1/4 in.

NAVIGATING AFRICA

THE IDEA WAS TO "PAVE" AN AERIAL PATH FROM PARIS TO FRENCH PROTECTORATE Madagascar—the large island off the southeastern coast of the African continent. By 1933 Madagascar was producing much of France's coffee supply and providing assorted natural resources. Maintaining a significant political influence on the African continent, however, was France's main motivation for forging an airway over one of the most inhospitable lands on Earth—North Africa's Sahara.

Working with Belgian airline Sabena, Régie Air Afrique was by 1936 offering flights to Brazzaville, capital of the French Congo (now the Republic of Congo in western Africa). When transporting passengers, most airlines in the '30s flew no higher than 6,000 feet. In Africa, flying low to the ground was vital because navigational aides, such as beacons, did not exist. Directives like "follow arrow traced in ground," "large rock, very visible," "to the right, rock shaped like pyramid" characterized the pilot's flight plan.

Along Régie Air Afrique's route from Algiers, in Algeria, to Brazzaville, strong winds and blowing sands above the Sahara could obscure the pilot's view, making landmarks such as rocks unrecognizable. In the south, depending on the flood stage of the Niger and Chari Rivers, cities in the central part of the route could be "very visible" on one flight and "not so visible" on another. Nonetheless, the pith-helmeted French bureaucrat in the poster at right confidently holds a map of French colonial Africa as if he were a modern-day Atlas.

AIR AFRIQUE
CIRCA 1936
39 1/2 x 24 1/2 in.

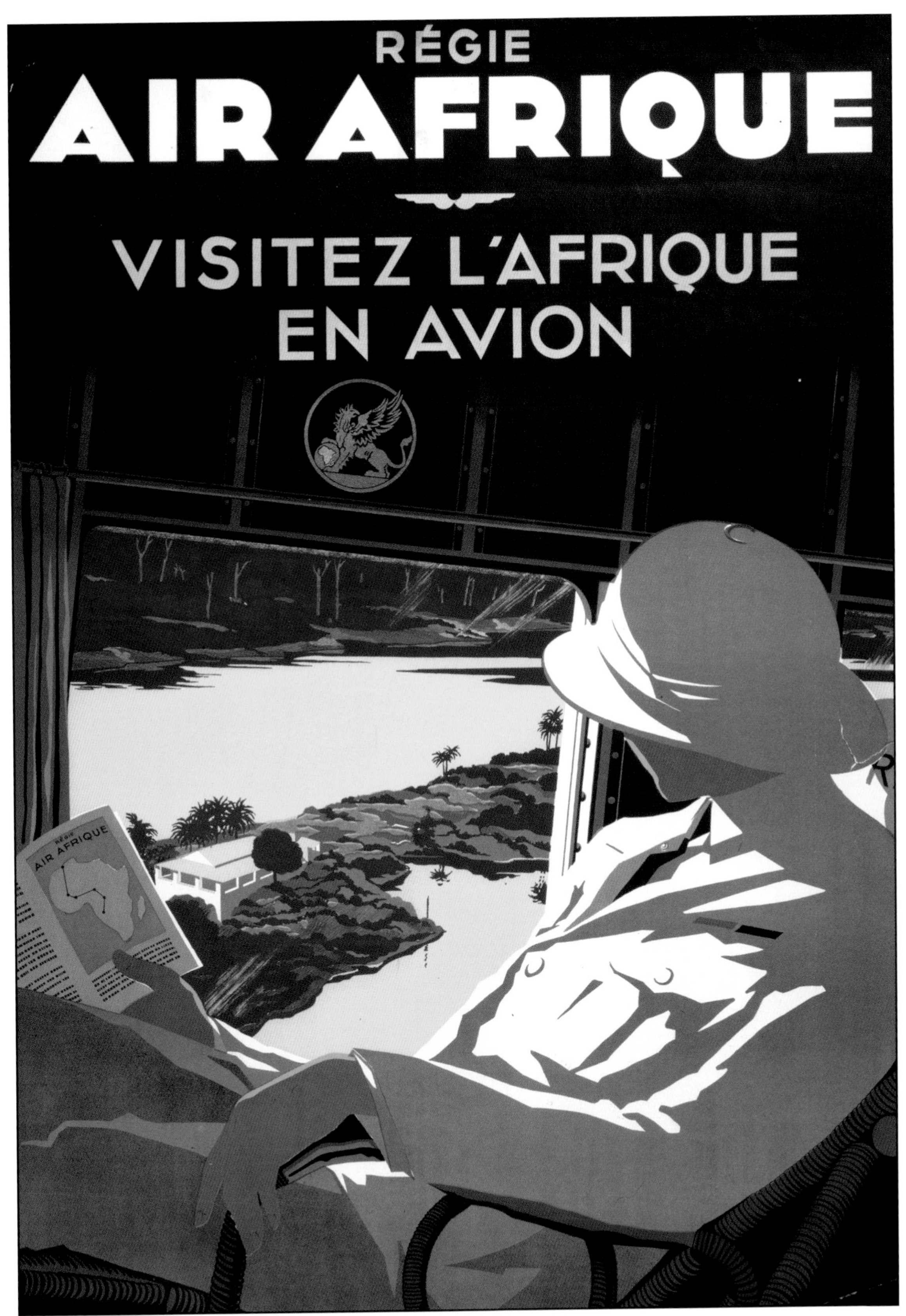
RÉGIE
AIR AFRIQUE
VISITEZ L'AFRIQUE
EN AVION
RÉGIE
AIR AFRIQUE

LUXURY

in the new Empire Flying-Boats

IMPERIAL AIRWAYS

EUROPE · AFRICA · INDIA · CHINA · AUSTRALIA

FEEL THE ADVANTAGE

The airline industry walked a fine line when it compared itself to the passenger train industry in order to sell its services. On the one hand, obvious differences made the message easy to deliver. By the mid-1930s airplanes were faster, cleaner, quieter, and more exclusive than trains. On the other hand, airplanes were not as safe as trains. Accounts of airplane crashes and lost pilots often appeared in newspapers around the world.

One way to calm passengers' fears about air travel was to declare airplane cabin amenities as comfortable as those on a train, if not more so. The poster for Imperial Airways at left takes that approach to the limit. The only tip that these passengers are in flight is a view of the horizon out the window, and the text at bottom that promotes "Luxury in the new Empire Flying-Boats" (Short S.23s). Otherwise, the cabin resembles a roomier version of a Pullman car, the ultimate in train travel at the time. As in a train's lounge car, women, children, young couples, and elderly matrons all travel comfortably. There is ample room for luggage above the seat, and an elegantly dressed steward brings refreshments. The message is clear: Grab your passport and luxury is yours—whether you are on the way to Africa, India, China, or Australia.

LUXURY
CIRCA 1938
19 1/2 x 12 1/2 in.

LINEA A[illegible]REA N[illegible]CIONAL

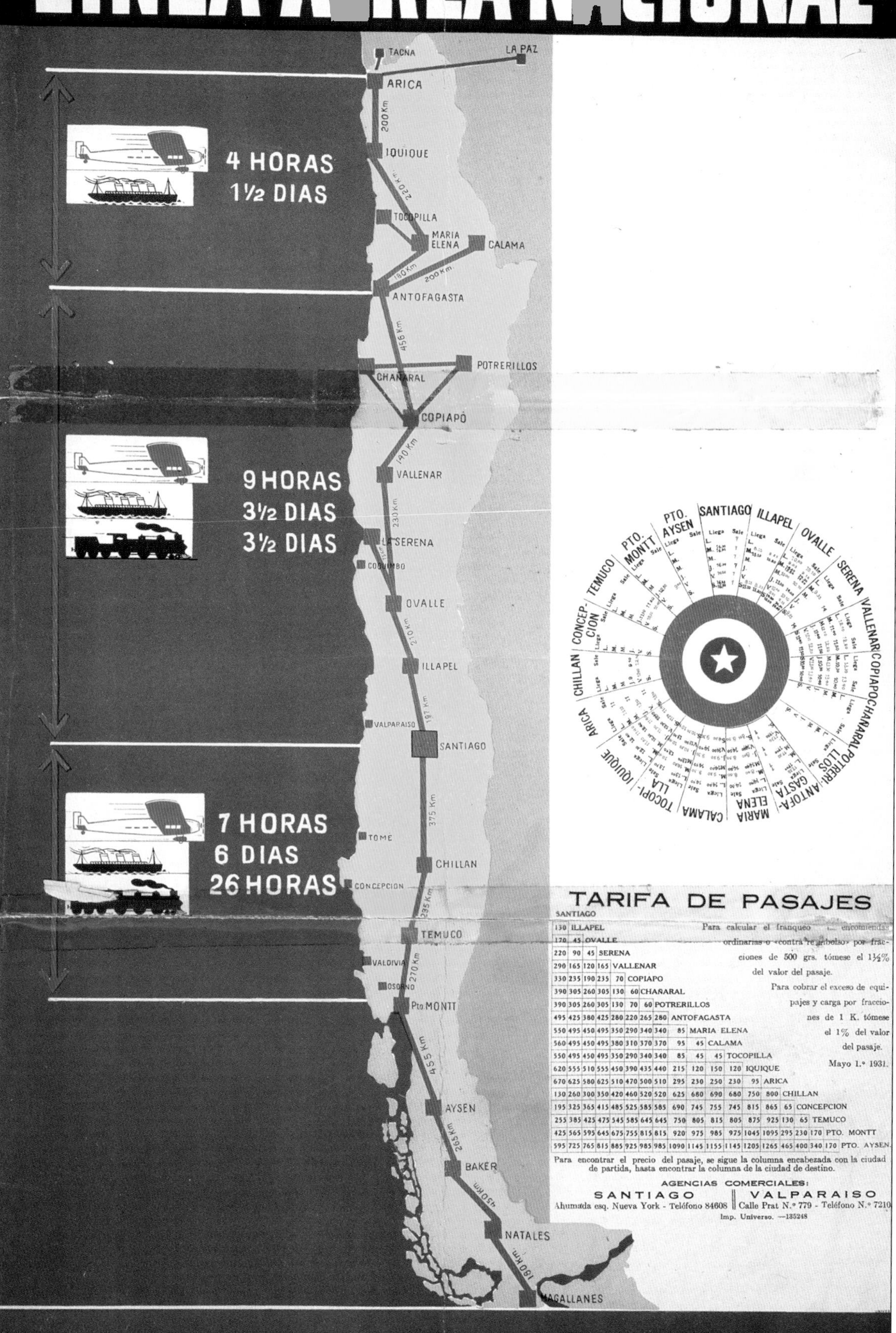

TARIFA DE PASAJES

SANTIAGO																		
130	ILLAPEL																	
170	45	OVALLE																
220	90	45	SERENA															
290	165	120	165	VALLENAR														
330	235	190	235	70	COPIAPO													
390	305	260	305	130	60	CHAÑARAL												
390	305	260	305	130	70	60	POTRERILLOS											
495	425	380	425	280	220	265	280	ANTOFAGASTA										
550	495	450	495	350	290	340	340	85	MARIA ELENA									
560	495	450	495	380	310	370	370	95	45	CALAMA								
550	495	450	495	350	290	340	340	85	45	45	TOCOPILLA							
620	555	510	555	450	390	435	440	215	120	150	120	IQUIQUE						
670	625	580	625	510	470	500	510	295	230	250	230	95	ARICA					
130	260	300	350	420	460	520	520	625	680	690	680	750	800	CHILLAN				
195	325	365	415	485	525	585	585	690	745	755	745	815	865	65	CONCEPCION			
255	385	425	475	545	585	645	645	750	805	815	805	875	925	130	65	TEMUCO		
425	565	595	645	675	755	815	815	920	975	985	975	1045	1095	295	230	170	PTO. MONTT	
595	725	765	815	885	925	985	985	1090	1145	1155	1145	1205	1265	465	400	340	170	PTO. AYSEN.

Para calcular el franqueo [illegible] encomiendas ordinarias o «contra reembolso» por fracciones de 500 grs. tómese el 1½% del valor del pasaje.

Para cobrar el exceso de equipajes y carga por fracciones de 1 K. tómese el 1% del valor del pasaje.

Mayo 1.° 1931.

Para encontrar el precio del pasaje, se sigue la columna encabezada con la ciudad de partida, hasta encontrar la columna de la ciudad de destino.

AGENCIAS COMERCIALES:

SANTIAGO — Ahumada esq. Nueva York - Teléfono 84608

VALPARAISO — Calle Prat N.° 779 - Teléfono N.° 7210

Imp. Universo. —135248

VIA - LINEA AEREA NACIONAL

LINKING A NATION

ACCORDING TO AVIATION HISTORIAN R. E.G. DAVIES, THE AIRPLANE PLAYED A unique and unprecedented role in the economic and cultural development of Latin America. Central and South America's deserts, jungles, and mountains had discouraged scattered settlement patterns and encouraged the growth of large, though disparate, urban centers. By the 1920s and '30s French- and German-based airlines raced to inaugurate scheduled flights between these large, isolated population centers and vied to supply aircraft to new local airlines in these areas. By the start of World War II, airlines large and small, local and foreign-based, served cities in Central America, the Caribbean, and South America.

In a long and mountainous nation such as Chile, the airplane played an especially important role in connecting the country. While U.S.-based Pan American-Grace Airways (formed in 1929) provided an international link, Linea Aérea Nacional (LAN), Chile's national carrier, had sole rights to air travel within the country. Originally a military-run airline, LAN became a commercial venture in 1929, offering faster, cheaper rates for transporting mail and people than did Chile's nationally subsidized railroad and shipping lines. By 1937 LAN flew from Santiago, the capital, in central Chile, to distant Antofogasta, on the northern coast, in nine hours—three days faster than by ship or train. The circular presentation of LAN's timetable in the poster shows connections between Arica, in the north, and Puerta Aysen, south of Santiago. LAN's circular rendition of the Chilean flag at the timetable's center reminds consumers of the airline's status as the national carrier.

LINEA AEREA NACIONAL
1937
19 1/2 x 12 in.

E. MAURUS
PARIS
LONDON
GOLDEN RAY
AIR UNION
PUBLIX · GERIN

EUROPE'S PRIME AIR ROUTE

1.

2.

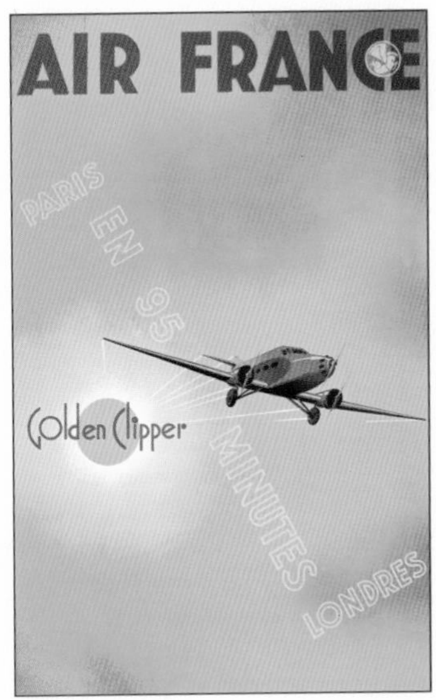

3.

By the late 1920s airlines began naming individual airplanes and giving monikers to particular services or routes. In 1927 Imperial Airways inaugurated its Silver Wing service between London and Paris, using Armstrong-Whitworth Argosy airplanes. Imperial named each Argosy after one of England's largest cities. Eventually Imperial introduced larger aircraft on the route and named these superior airplanes after mythological and historical figures rather than place-names.

In 1929, to compete with England's Silver Wing service, French airline Air Union began flying Lioré and Olivier LeO21s (1) on the Paris-London route, which they named the Golden Ray (2). In 1933 Air France (3) inherited Air Union's Paris-London route but used speedier Wibault 282s. The Golden Clipper's Wibaults were so fast they "clipped" 30 minutes off the Golden Ray's flight times.

GOLDEN RAY; GOLDEN CLIPPER
1929; 1933
39 1/2 x 24 1/4 in.;.39 1/2 x 24 1/2 in.

FLYG MED
A-B AEROTRANSPORT

FEEL THE POWER

Technology played a starring role in airline posters created in the post-WWI years. Airline publicity agents made sure the public took note when an airline introduced to its fleet an aircraft with a more powerful engine, a sleeker design, and the ability to fly a greater distance.

Swedish artist Anders Beckman's poster at left, created for A.B. Aerotransport, Sweden's national carrier, is a snapshot of anticipation, and a precursor of the artist's later work in which he combined photography with graphics. The Fokker F.XII speeding into the poster at top left counterpoints the static scene below. Beckman captures the nervous excitement shared by many airline passengers at the moment of boarding: The passengers wait in line—one looking forward, perhaps, to finding a seat, and the other looking back, maybe reconsidering her decision to fly. Revving engines rotate the propellers at such speed that the artist can only illustrate the space they circumscribe. At the bottom of the poster, solid, three-dimensional, yellow type appears like chocks, stopping the forward motion of the giant tire in the foreground. Despite the speed and noise the image depicts, the imposing goliath-size airplane is inviting. Beckman's design is deceptively simple—an appealing and accessible picture of the complexities of flight.

FLYG
1932
39 1/2 x 24 1/2 in.

AN *ENSIGN* AIR LINER FOR EMPIRE SERVICES

2 DECKS 200 M.P.H. 20 TONS

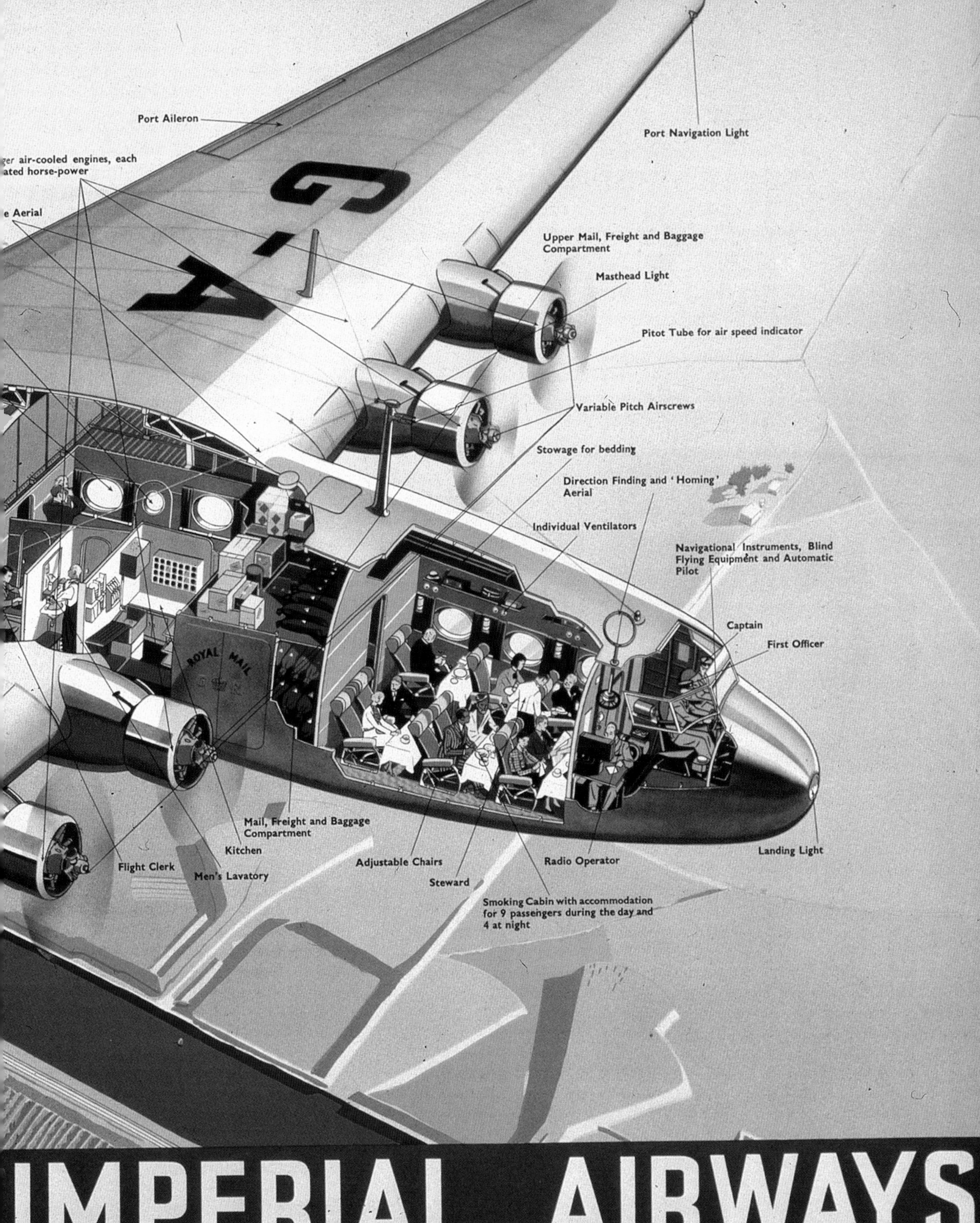

Port Aileron
Port Navigation Light
ger air-cooled engines, each
ated horse-power
e Aerial
G-A
Upper Mail, Freight and Baggage Compartment
Masthead Light
Pitot Tube for air speed indicator
Variable Pitch Airscrews
Stowage for bedding
Direction Finding and 'Homing' Aerial
Individual Ventilators
Navigational Instruments, Blind Flying Equipment and Automatic Pilot
Captain
First Officer
ROYAL MAIL
Mail, Freight and Baggage Compartment
Kitchen
Flight Clerk
Men's Lavatory
Adjustable Chairs
Steward
Radio Operator
Landing Light
Smoking Cabin with accommodation for 9 passengers during the day and 4 at night
IMPERIAL AIRWAYS
EUROPE • AFRICA • INDIA • THE FAR EAST • AUSTRALIA • BERMUDA • NEW YORK

SUPER TECHNOLOGY

AIRLINE POSTERS OF THIS ERA PROMISED FASTER, LARGER, MORE EFFICIENT, OR more comfortable aircraft, as touted in the poster's gigantic cutaway on the previous pages. Another technique artists used to emphasize this point in the mid-1930s was showing the size of an airline's fleet. Even though airlines never flew passenger flights in formation, as in the poster at right, such imagery suggests that the airline flew frequent flights and used the most modern technology. In the case of flag carriers, such advertising implied that a technologically strong nation was a modern political and economic force.

In 1933, Italy's minister for air Italo Balbo organized and led two spectacular mass international flights to demonstrate Italy's air power. In 1931, Balbo headed a fleet of seaplanes (12 Savoia Marchetti SM.55s) from Rome to Rio de Janeiro; then in 1933, he led a fleet of 24 Savoia Marchetti SM.55s from Rome to New York City and then Chicago. Awed crowds met the flyers in Rio, New York, and Chicago. Balbo returned to Italy as a national hero. Artists Luigi Martinati and Umberto di Lazzaro created posters to commemorate his flights. Martinati's 1933 poster shows a bridge, composed of seaplanes, joining New York City and Rome.

The 1936 Japan Air Transport (JAT) poster at right, featuring lines of DC-2s, resembles Luigi Martinati's poster. That year JAT introduced Douglas DC-2s to its fleet. Despite the poster's dramatic image, the airline never flew more than six DC-2s.

PREVIOUS PAGES: AN ENSIGN AIR LINER
1938
25 x 40 in.

In 1938 Imperial Airways introduced its Armstrong Whitworth A.W. 27 Ensign to compete with the Douglas DC-2 flown by other European airlines. James Gardner's poster (on pages 102-103) features a cutaway view of the Ensign. Imperial's artists often used this kind of illustration to introduce new aircraft. Although the Ensign was never a success, this detailed depiction of the airplane flying over a ship as it traversed the Suez Canal subtly promotes the airline's potential competitive edge. Callouts draw attention to the automatic pilot, variable-pitch propellers, and other technological advances. But because the public associated Imperial with luxury, the poster works more to reassure veteran customers that designing for speed had not lowered Imperial's high standards of in-flight amenities. The cutaway shows passengers lounging or smoking in the cozy atmosphere of the cocoonlike cabin or "promenading" on the small deck between the kitchen and the men's sleeping quarters.

This JAT poster announces the Japanese national airline's super express service. One of its routes linked Tokyo to the capital of Manchuria (which Japan occupied in 1931).

SUPER EXPRESS IN THE SKY
1936
42 x 29 1/2 in..

Soc·An·
Aero Espresso Italiana
BRINDISI ATENE STAMBOUL
PASSEGGERI · POSTA · MERCI
Rivolgetevi alle principali agenzie di viaggi

PEWAS
DERULUFT
HELSINKI
LENINGRAD
TALLINN
RIGA
MOSKVA
WELIKIJE LUKI
KAUNAS
KÖNIGSBERG
DANZIG
LONDON
AMSTERDAM
BERLIN
BRÜSSEL
PARIS
BERLIN·MOSKAU·LENINGRAD

NOW YOU CAN SPEND
ALL YOUR VACATION ..
FISHING
WORLD'S FINEST
FISHING GROUNDS
JUST A FEW HOURS
AWAY ON
The Great Silver Fleet
EASTERN AIR LINES

LEE-ELLIOTT
LONDON
AND
LE TOUQUET
IN ONE
FLYING
HOUR
BY
IMPERIAL
AIRWAYS
FOR TIMES & FARES

TIME MACHINES

WHILE SCIENTISTS IN THE 1930S WERE DEVELOPING NEW MODELS OF THE physical world based on their growing understanding of the atom, airline marketers were commissioning posters like these at left that suggested that the airplane had changed travelers' perception of speed, time, and distance.

Giuseppe Riccobaldi's poster, top left, for Aero Espresso Italiano (AEI) features a seaplane rising from the dome of Istanbul's Hagia Sophia, flying over the Parthenon in Athens, and then swooping past columns marking the end of the Roman-built Appian Way. In this quick trip through history, AEI transcends its role as a mere mode of transportation and becomes a fantastic time machine.

In 1922 German-Russian airline Deruluft offered flights between Berlin and Moscow, adding Leningrad in 1928. German artist Peter Pewas created a poster, top right, that aimed to illustrate the airlines' claim that "the eye will pass over . . . countries like the finger over a map." The diagonal lines and typography promise velocity, as the arrowlike airplane speeds toward Moscow.

The Imperial Airways and Eastern Air Lines posters, bottom right and left, equate time, distance, and speed. In the Imperial poster, artist Theyre Lee-Elliott reduces the idea of distance to the image of a clock face, advertising the one-hour flight from London to Le Touquet, a French resort. The Eastern poster urges sportsmen and -women to patronize the Great Silver Fleet and "spend *all* [their] vacation . . . fishing" in "the world's finest fishing grounds" in Florida.

AEI; DERULUFT; IMPERIAL AIRWAYS; FISHING
1931; 1934; 1933; 1937
13 1/4 x 9 1/2 in.; 26 1/4 x 18 in.; 12 x 8 1/2 in.; 19 1/8 x 13 7/8 in.

REGULAR SERVICES

PARIS

2½ HRS.

JERSEY

FLY ANYTIME

Building infrastructure, such as airports, allowed airlines to offer regular, reliable service. But in the early days of the aviation industry, some lines, like Jersey Airways, operated without airports, using fields or beaches. Connecting Paris and London with Jersey—the southernmost of Britain's Channel Islands and located just 12 miles west of France—the airline flew more than 20,000 passengers in 1934.

Before Jersey Airways began service to the island in 1933, airlines flew Super Marine Sea Eagle and Short S.8 Calcutta flying boats, landing on St. Aubin's Bay. By contrast, Jersey Airways flew landplanes—de Havilland D.H.84 Dragons—and landed on West Park Beach next to the bay. Jersey Airways service was as regular as the tides—which submerged this makeshift airport twice a day. Arrivals and departures must have been exciting for the passengers on Jersey Airways's six-seater airplanes, as well as for any sightseers lounging by the bay. Without a permanent landing strip, policemen cleared the beach when airplanes approached and cordoned off a temporary runway with rope. Shifting sands, however, did not deter vacationers from visiting the sunny island, and in 1938 Jersey opened its airport.

JERSEY AIRWAYS
CIRCA 1932
40 x 25 in.

THE CHRISTMAS EXPRESS

AIRPORTS, TWO-WAY RADIO SYSTEMS, AN ARRAY OF LIGHTED BEACONS, AND more had to be developed and built before airlines could fly regularly at night, in the winter, or reliably through inclement weather. Even before World War I, engineers had begun to investigate new methods to improve airplane systems. During the 1930s aeronautical engineers developed a series of instruments, including altimeters, radio transmitters, and receivers, that allowed pilots to keep their airplanes on track even in the worst of storms. Developments on the ground also improved air safety. Airports were constructed to cater to the increase in air traffic. Landing strips were lighted, and the first air traffic controllers began using colored flags to communicate with pilots preparing to land. Eventually these controllers moved into radio towers, from which they transmitted information about weather conditions to pilots and directed air traffic to and from the ground.

In 1933 American's Lockheed Orion in the poster at right gave a propeller-driven boost to Santa's reindeer during the Christmas season. An extensive system of high-powered electric beacons, emergency landing strips, and wireless stations—not the Star of Bethlehem, as the poster implies—allowed American's pilots to fly through the night from coast to coast. The poster's serene, snowy, rural landscape featuring farmhouse and church was designed to tug at heartstrings, and may have opened more wallets than did the small print promising delivery to "cities 1,000 to 3,000 miles away."

"OF COURSE, BY AEROPLANE"

THE CZECH AIRLINE ČESKOSLOVENSKÁ LETECKÁ SPOLEÃNOST (CLS) PRINTED THE poster at left in German, French, and English. The English version might have been intended for the airline's passengers hailing from London, a new destination for the airline in 1937. One year later the company produced a brochure that showcased the Prague-London route as evidence that during the airline's ten-year history the airplane had become as indispensable to a modern businessman as the typewriter and the telephone. On the last page of this brochure, a man holds a telephone earpiece close. The accompanying text allows us to listen in on his conversation: "London? Here Prague. . . . Yes, I shall be in London within five hours. Please prepare all, for I must be back in Prague tomorrow midday . . . of course, by aeroplane."

The poster suggests that ČLS aircraft offered not only speed, at the rate of the winged god Mercury, but also security and comfort. Even the most progressive traveler might doubt if an airline could guarantee a godlike level of protection. Still, the company brochure insisted that ČLS passengers would find the airplanes both powerful and reliable. The poster touts the security, speed, and comfort trifecta, and the brochure elaborates the point. Detailed drawings illustrate improvements in aircraft radio technology and beacons, which allowed ČLS pilots to navigate through storms. And, with a more powerful fleet, pilots could comfortably soar over the Alps with 1,500 meters (about 5,000 feet) to spare!

CZECHOSLOVAK AIR TRANSPORT COMPANY
1938
38 x 24 1/2 in.

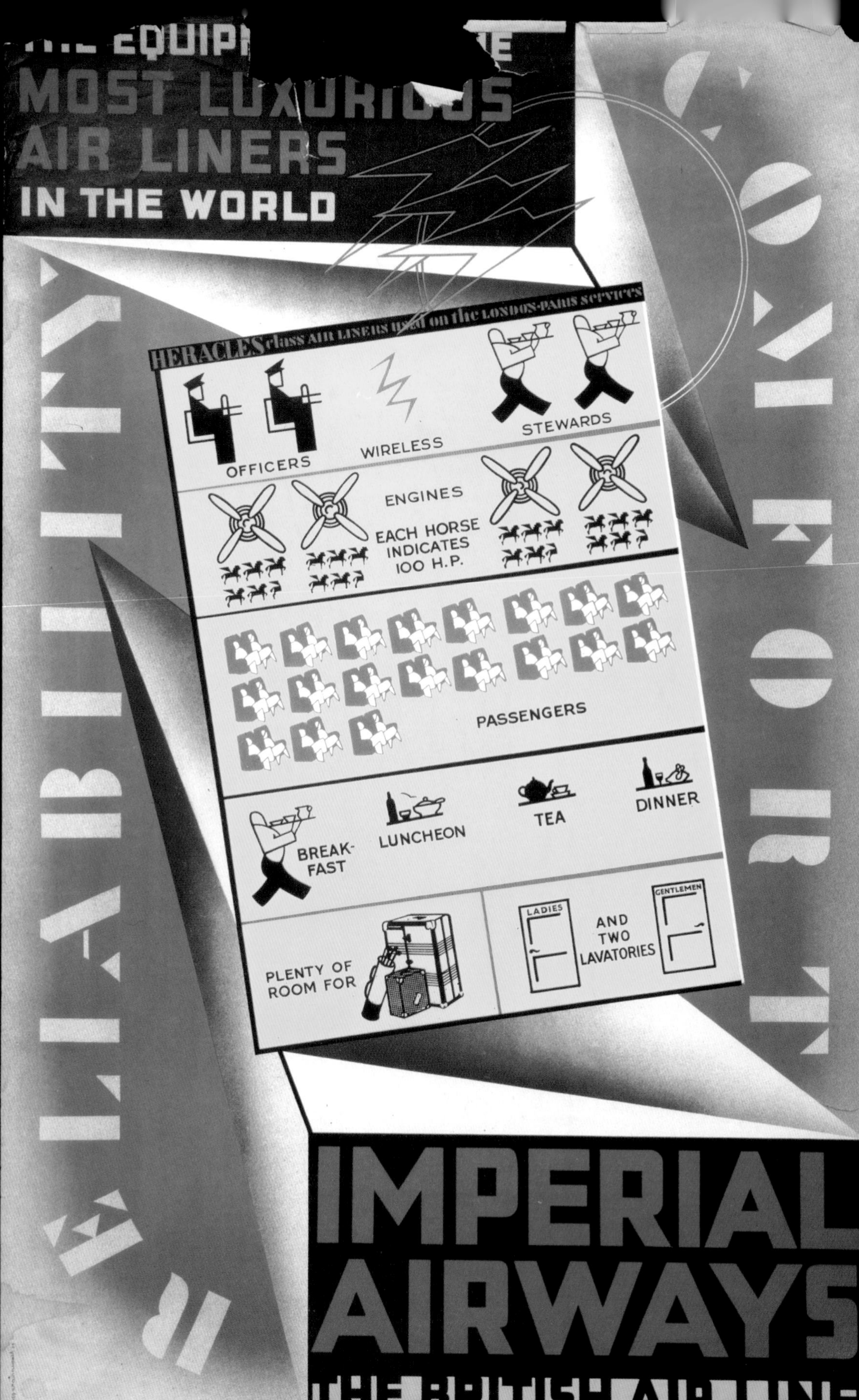

MOST LUXURIOUS
AIR LINERS
IN THE WORLD
RELIABILITY
COMFORT
HERACLES class AIR LINERS used on the LONDON-PARIS services
OFFICERS
WIRELESS
STEWARDS
ENGINES
EACH HORSE INDICATES 100 H.P.
PASSENGERS
BREAK-FAST
LUNCHEON
TEA
DINNER
PLENTY OF ROOM FOR
LADIES
GENTLEMEN
AND TWO LAVATORIES
IMPERIAL
AIRWAYS
THE BRITISH AIR LINE

INSPIRING CONFIDENCE

The poster at left quintessentially illustrates the challenge of designing advertising for aviation in the early 1930s. This most modern technology warranted the use of the latest graphic art techniques—but artists had to keep in mind that most of their audience had yet to fly.

British artist Edgar Ainsworth's poster composition is a well-balanced combination of two avant-garde styles. Ainsworth's edgy chevrons imply speed and modernity even if they misrepresent the performance of the pokey aircraft Imperial used on its European routes. But the words "Reliability" and "Comfort" accurately reflect Imperial's Handley Page H.P. 42 airplanes, which offered plush seating, restaurant-quality meals, and engines damped to allow normal conversation.

To detail the airplane's amenities, Ainsworth shifted gears and used a different design technique, choosing a more direct and illustrative but still avant-garde approach to present these facts. He used symbols—propellers, horses, and half horses, for example—to represent the plane's four 555-horsepower engines. If this storefront poster did not convince travelers to fly Imperial, timetables available at the agent's desk inside the airline's ticket office offered presumably convincing rationales: Using the airline's safety record as a selling point, copy read, "It is so safe to travel by Imperial Airways that practically no Assurance Company calls for an additional premium on your Life Assurance."

RELIABILITY COMFORT
1934
40 x 25 in.

IM WINTER WIRD GEFLOGEN

DEUTSCHE LUFT HANSA A.G.

AUSKUNFT UND FLUGSCHEINE IN ALLEN REISEBÜROS

A WHOLE NEW WORLD

Noted Swiss graphic designer Herbert Matter used photographs with typography and hand-drawn elements to create innovative images for the Swiss Tourist Bureau in the 1930s. Layering and juxtaposing photographs taken from unusual perspectives, Matter made the ancient Alps and its resorts look modern.

The poster at left by Werner Weiskonig, a contemporary of Matter, shows how well Matter's stylistic innovations especially suited advertisements for aviation. Every time passengers took an airplane trip they saw familiar sites from a new, striking perspective—from miles above the ground and through the frame of an airplane window. Weiskonig used enlarged aerial photographs of cities along East Swiss Airline's route—instead of the colored dot conventially used by mapmakers—to indicate place. The route map fills the page and floats in the sky, detached from any other point of reference. An airplane silhouette provides space for text and flies above the route map, adding yet another element of movement to the poster. Nevertheless, Weiskonig's composition is easy to read and at the same time captures the disorienting experience that flying often induced.

FLIEGT
CIRCA 1933
28 1/4 x 39 1/4 in.

TWICE WEEKLY SERVICE
1934
28 1/4 x 39 1/4 in.

"1/3 OF THE EARTH'S CIRCUMFERENCE"

KLM Royal Dutch Airlines had a head start over other national carriers. In 1919, five years before Imperial Airways was even founded, KLM pilots began to fly Fokker F.IIs from Amsterdam to London. In 1924 KLM made a proving flight from Amsterdam to Batavia (now Jakarta), capital of the Dutch East Indies (now Indonesia), a flight of 7,053 miles. In 1929 KLM launched regular service between the Netherlands and its Southeast Asian colony.

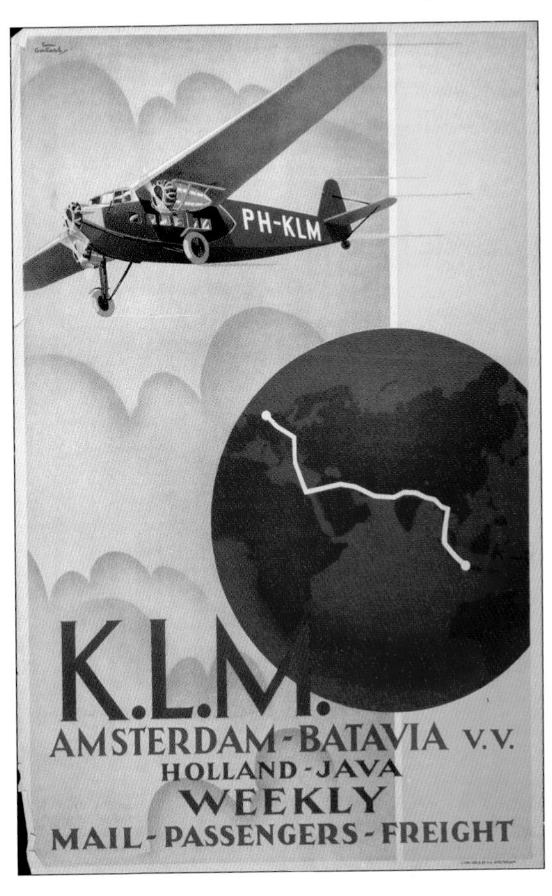

In 1931 KLM flew 12-seat F.XIIs on its Amsterdam-Batavia route. By 1934 KLM planned to use a 36-seat Fokker, offering twice-weekly service.

KLM traveled far on the wings of Dutch manufacturer and aircraft designer Anthony Fokker's aircraft. As KLM expanded, Fokker designed new airplanes. In 1931 KLM used the Fokker F.XII, above. KLM planned to use the new F.XXXVI at left on the same route by 1934. But by the time the first and only model was ready, the airline had decided to use more efficient Douglas DC-2s along its route.

RED GLOBE, KLM
CIRCA 1931
11 7/8 x 7 1/2 in.

VH-ABB
VH-ABC
LONDON
SYDNEY
Fly British across the world
QANTAS EMPIRE AIRWAYS
IN ASSOCIATION WITH IMPERIAL AIRWAYS

CHAPTER FOUR

MORE PRODUCTION

1939–1955

From the global connector of peacetime in the 1930s, the airplane was transformed into a weapon of war when World War II broke out in Europe in 1939. Germany joined forces with Italy to conquer Europe. In the Pacific, Japan joined these powers that became known as the Axis. All these nation's leaders had been visionaries of air power, and their air forces were formidable. To stop the Axis advance, Britain and other powers fought as the Allied forces. They brought their own daunting air power to the theaters of war in Europe and the Pacific. As the war progressed, airplanes became a daily presence in the lives of most people around the world. Combat aircraft taking off from aircraft carriers in the Pacific gave the advantage to the Allies—and prepared the way for the defeat of Japan. By 1945, bombers in Europe and in Japan had finished the job.

Posters played a role in educating the public about wartime aviation. Shortly after the United States entered the war, after the Japanese

MORE PRODUCTION
1942
40 x 28 in.

bombing of Pearl Harbor in 1941, the Office of Civilian Defense enlisted the Boy Scouts of America to dispatch to American citizens five million posters describing what to do in case of an air raid.

In the U.S., commercial airlines continued to operate during the war, but with greatly diminished fleets. The U.S. Army and Navy Air Forces took possession of up to 75 percent of some airlines' inventory. Many airline pilots left civilian life to enlist. Pilots from the Women's Auxiliary Ferrying Squadron (WAFS), Women's Army Auxiliary Corps (WAAC), and Civil Air Patrol (CAP) stepped up to help the war effort.

The Office of Defense Transportation ensured that airline marketing programs did not encourage unnecessary flying; conversely, airline marketing departments made sure the public knew that the airlines contributed to the war effort. A 1942 print ad for Trans World Airlines (TWA) epitomized the approach, applauding the nation's airlines as being "indispensable" to efforts on the home front—"where every minute gained is a victory won."

After the war ended in 1945, airline marketers took another tack: They proclaimed the importance of aviation to the postwar world. Airline officials unveiled new craft with technology developed before or during the war but not available to commercial aviation until afterward. TWA's signature Lockheed Constellation ("Connie"), with its distinctive three-finned tail, (in poster at right) was one such debutante. The tail's innovative design balanced the unusually long fuselage. On May 6, 1946, TWA launched the Connie's international service with a New York-to-Paris flight. Comfortable seats converted into beds, stewardesses served hot food, and a cocktail lounge beckoned.

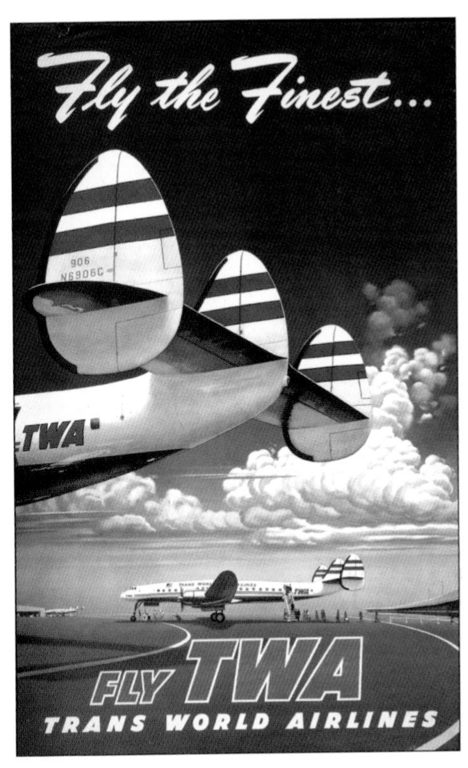

TWA's Lockheed Constellation Super Connie was easy to identify with its dipped nose, triple tail, and elegant, elongated fuselage.

Like the Connie's tail, the jet engine was a prewar design that came into its own after the war. In the late 1920s and early '30s, British engineer Frank Whittle and German engineer Hans von Ohain independently designed the world's first jet engines. The British and German militaries began developing air frames to use the innovative engine, and by 1944 both nations were flying jet-powered fighters. After the war, British engineers applied this technology to build airliners with jet engines. In 1952, British Overseas Airways Corporation (BOAC) began flying the de Havilland Comet, the world's first jet airliner.

FLY THE FINEST
1952
40 x 25 in.

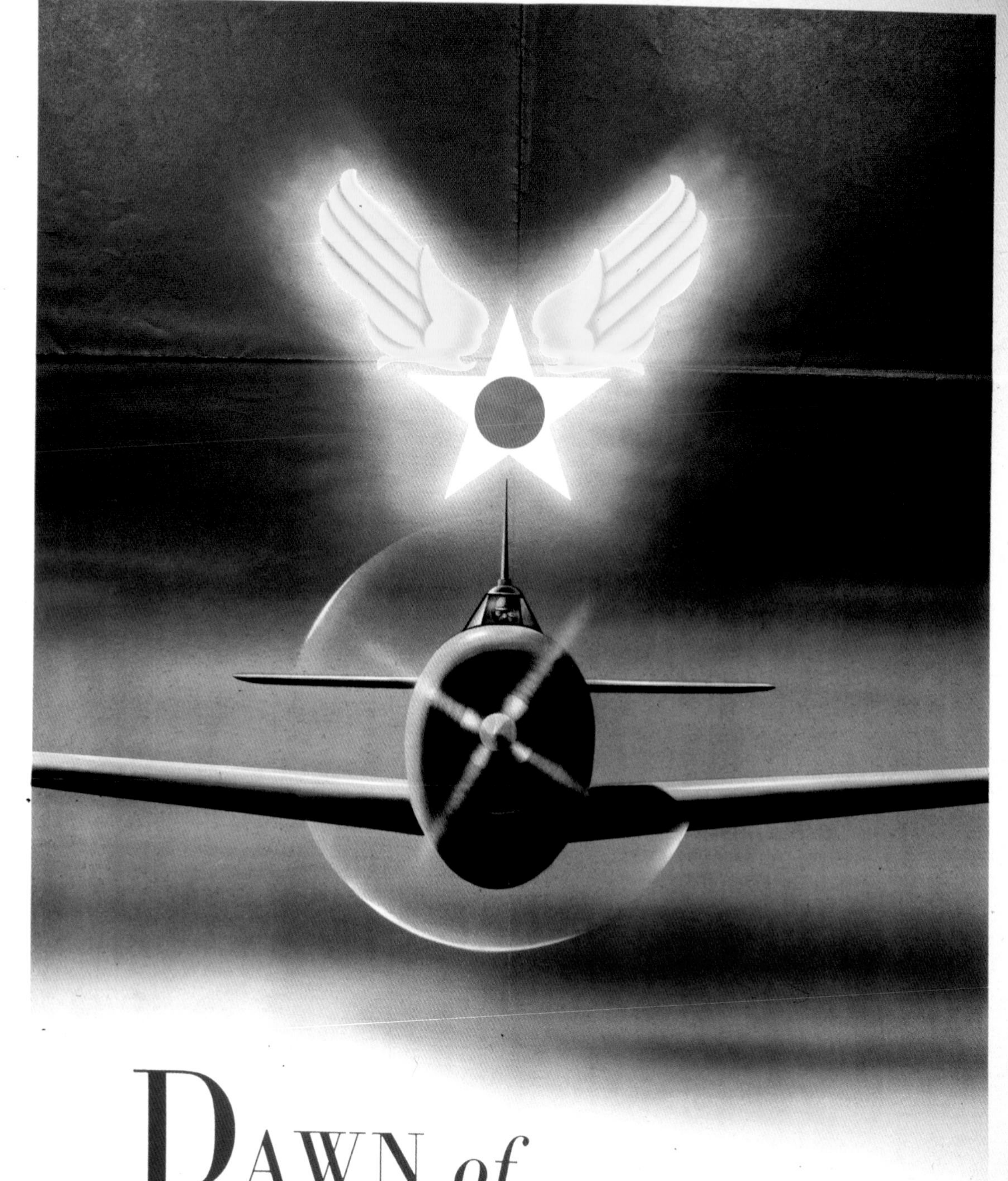
DAWN of
YOUR FUTURE
U. S. ARMY AIR FORCES
—Enlist Today!

THE "YOU" IN WWII

The nose of the Republic P-47 fighter airplane in the 1945 poster at left flies directly out of the page at prospective U.S. Army Air Forces (USAAF) recruits. The airplane, a symbol of USAAF might, was itself a compelling reason for young men to enlist in this service. The USAAF insignia above the P-47 offered an image that U.S. citizens recognized. The insignia's golden wings—sometimes referred to as the "Hap Arnold" wings in honor of charismatic Air Forces commander Gen. Henry "Hap" Arnold—and star meant duty, glamour, and victory. The poster helped to recruit the pilots needed right up to the end of World War II and after, to replace the nearly two million airmen who left the service at the end of 1945.

This poster's emphasis on "your future" was typical of posters made for home front consumption. They sold the idea that every person—even those far from the fighting—played a vital role in winning the war. Before WWII, only a fraction of Americans had flown. The war profoundly changed that. By the end of the war, many men and women had been given an opportunity to fly or work in the aviation industry. As a result, the U.S. was signficantly more air-minded, with a surplus of pilots, aircraft, and mechanics.

DAWN OF YOUR FUTURE
1945
38 x 25 in.

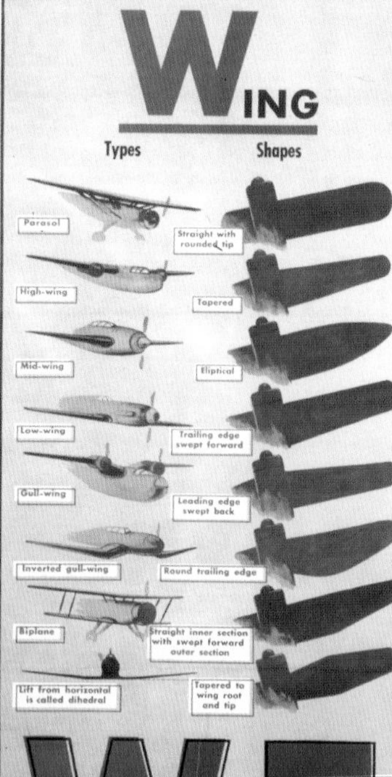

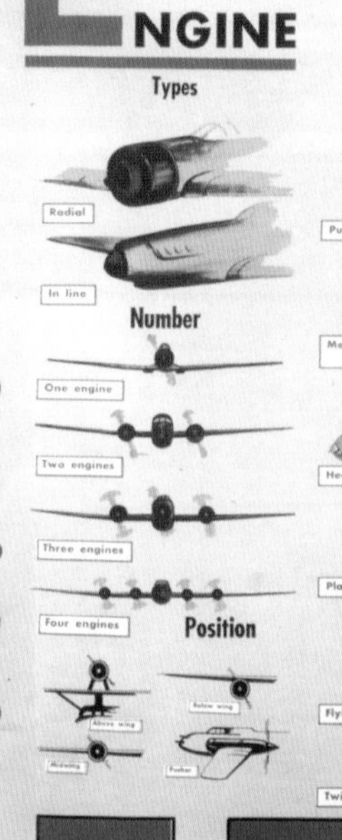

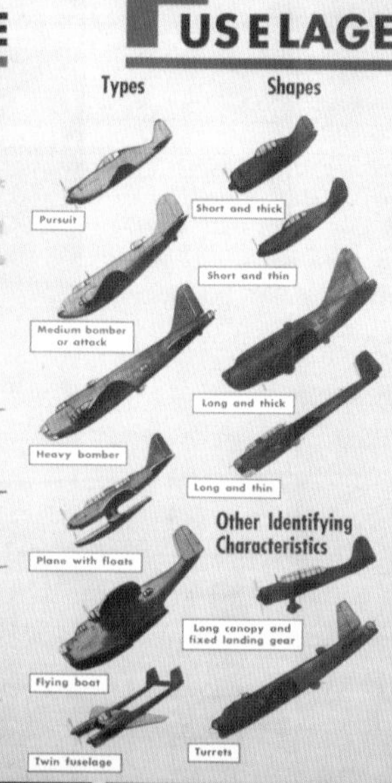

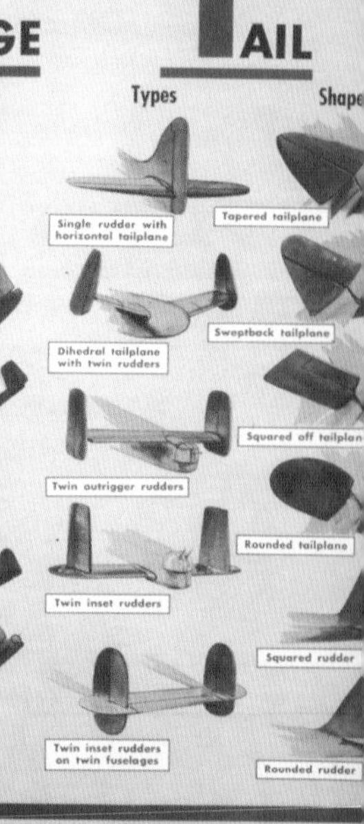

WEFT
1942
37 3/4 x 47 in.

IDENTIFYING AIRCRAFT

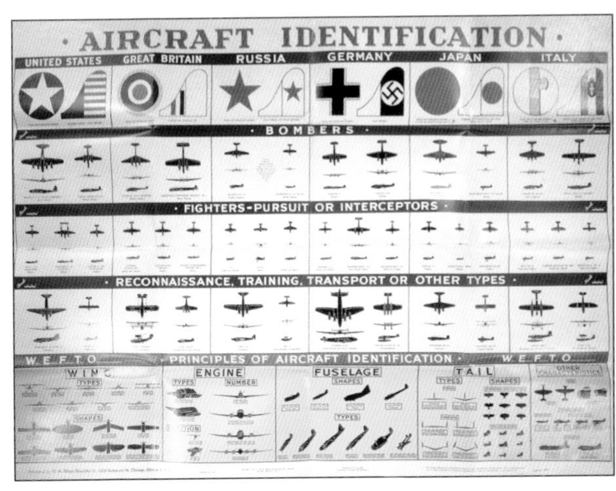

Aircraft identification posters hung in schoolrooms, military training facilities, and airplane spotters' cabins.

For most Americans, learning to identify airplanes for the U.S. government was their first experience with aviation. Japan's attack on Pearl Harbor in 1941 had left the U.S. government fearful of such an attack on the U.S. mainland—and airplane spotting soon became a serious endeavor. The poster at left shows the WEFT (Wings, Engine, Fuselage, Tail) recognition system used by spotters.

As well as distributing posters for the Office of Civilian Defense, Boy Scouts across the nation helped to raise money to build spotters' cabins in fields and isolated areas—and to act as spotters themselves. Spotters identified and reported any suspicious flying object. Husbands and wives worked together to observe and record every airplane heard and seen on two- to four-hour shifts, day and night. In addition, soon after the U.S. entered the war, women began to play a major role in aerial photograph reading and airplane identification using the WEFT system. In the summer of 1942, Indiana University began a Women's Auxiliary Training Corps class, teaching topics such as military first aid and theory and practice in the care and operation of motor vehicles.

AIRCRAFT IDENTIFICATION
1942
42 x 58 in.

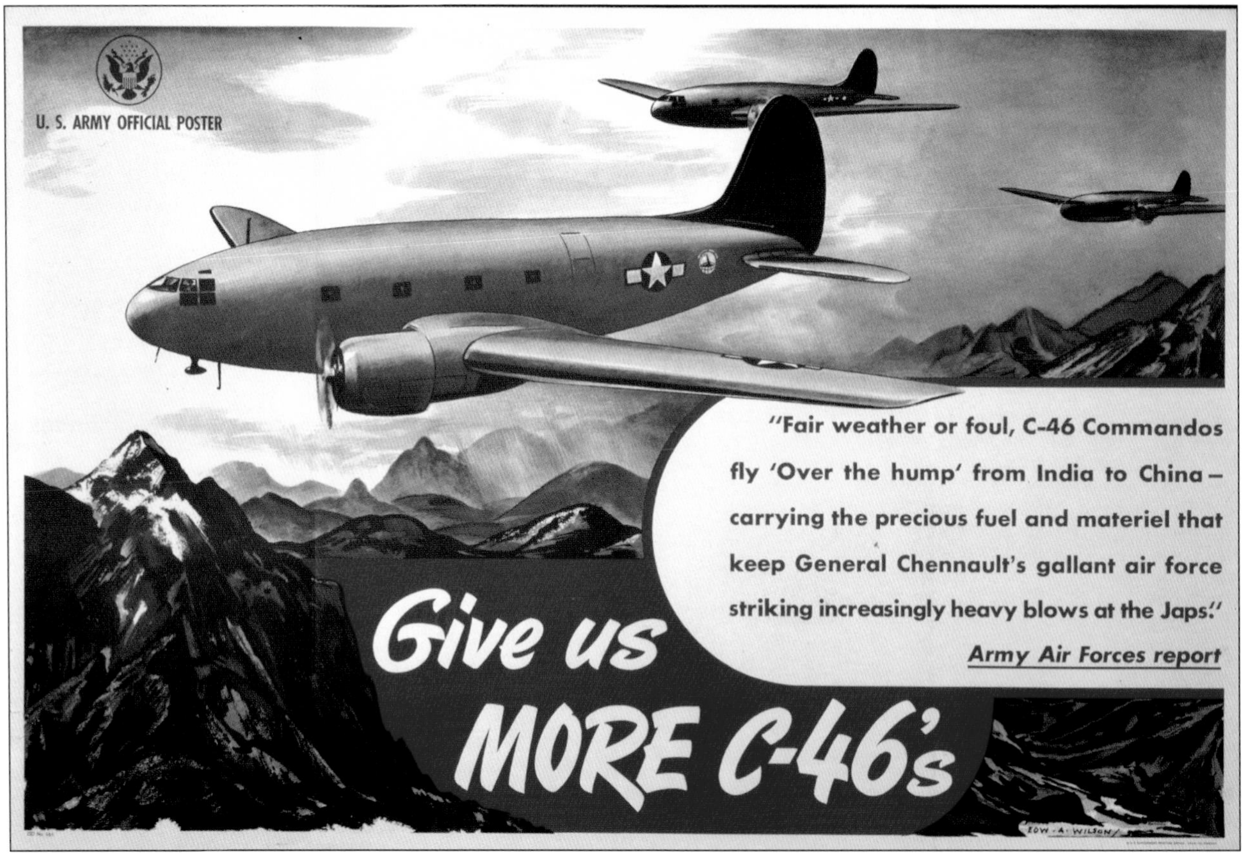

U. S. ARMY OFFICIAL POSTER

"Fair weather or foul, C-46 Commandos fly 'Over the hump' from India to China—carrying the precious fuel and materiel that keep General Chennault's gallant air force striking increasingly heavy blows at the Japs."

Army Air Forces report

Give us MORE C-46's

EDW. A. WILSON

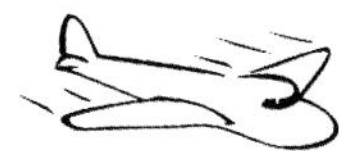

THE CHOSEN INSTRUMENTS

Airline companies, Army Air Corps reservists, the Women's Air Force Service Pilots (WASP), and the Civilian Pilot Training Program (CPTP) gave the Air Transport Command (ATC) more airplanes and more pilots. Essentially a military-run airline, the ATC played a crucial role in WWII "moving men and materiél," using transport airplanes including C-46s and C-54s, as in the posters at left. By 1944, WASPs working for the ATC were training pilots and testing fighters and bombers. Pilots in aircraft marked with the ATC emblem and the U.S. Army Air Force "star and bars" navigated new routes over the Atlantic and Pacific as well as across Asia's Himalayan range. Pan American Airways, the "chosen instrument" for U.S. international aviation, was serving the war effort even before Pearl Harbor. But other U.S. airlines were not far behind. The government assigned zones to the ATC, giving, for example, the North Atlantic zone to Pan Am, TWA, and Northeast. By war's end, the ATC had contracted with many airlines, and the airlines' response paid off: After the war, the government gave traffic rights to American, Northwest, and Braniff to serve Europe, Asia, and Latin America—taking away Pan Am's "chosen instrument" status.

C-46s; C-54s; COMMANDO
1944; 1944; 1943
25 x 38 in.; 38 x 25 in.; 38 x 25 in.

1944
1984
ICAO·OACI·ИКАО

CONTROLLING INTERNATIONAL AIRSPACE

BETWEEN THE WORLD WARS INTERNATIONAL AGREEMENTS FORMED BY MANY national carriers with foreign governments had been a key component of civil aviation progress: Dutch KLM, the first to fly long-distance routes, could only have done so with Britain's approval for it to land in India and other British colonies; until the mid-1920s, Germany refused fly-over rights to national carriers whose governments had signed the Versailles Treaty—limiting German aviation.

During World War II, military and commercial pilots rerouted airplanes as Allied and Axis powers gained or lost territory. Instead of renegotiating rights to airspace to accommodate these changes, nations allied with the U.S. allowed American airplanes unhampered access to their airspace. The Allies depended heavily on American aviation during the war. Once combat ended, however, Allied nations were quick to regain sovereignty of their airspaces, in order to foster homegrown civil aviation efforts. While the U.S. supported an "open skies" policy—airspace belonging to all nations—other countries, especially Great Britain, feared a U.S. civil aviation juggernaut. In Chicago, representatives from 54 countries, including the U.S. and Great Britain, met to discuss the creation of an international organization that would codify the rules of the sky. Fifty-two countries signed an agreement creating the International Civil Aviation Organization (ICAO) in 1944. The new organization would coordinate civil aviation activities, determining rules and rights to fly over or land in

PREVIOUS PAGES: ICAO
1984
17 1/2 x 24 in.

a foreign country. The commemorative poster on pages 140-141, designed in 1984, celebrates ICAO's 40 years as arbiter of the airways. It features the flight of Daedalus and his son Icarus, figures in Greek myth.

After WWII, as more U.S. airlines began to fly internationally, air travel became less novel. Soon marketers were creating ads, such as the Pan American poster at right, focusing on the charms of the destination rather than of the airplane itself. Fighting competition on its international routes, Pan Am billed itself as the "world's most experienced airline," and changed its name to Pan Am World Airways. Decades later in 1984, Pan Am, unable to bear the competition, was moving toward bankruptcy. The story of its founder, Juan Trippe, seemed to mirror that of Icarus. According to myth, Daedalus fashioned wings of feathers and wax for himself and Icarus. He warned Icarus not to fly too close to the sun—or the wax would melt. Trippe, too, overextended. By 1990 Pan Am was defunct.

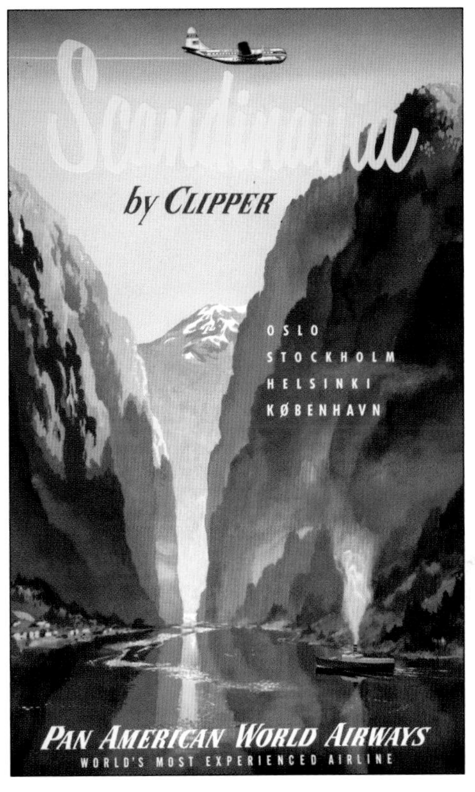

Pan Am began flying Boeing 377 Stratocruisers in 1949. Amenities, such as a two-level passenger cabin and a cocktail lounge, drew passengers who could afford to fly in comfort.

SCANDINAVIA
CIRCA 1951
40 x 25 in.

New York
UNITED
UNITED AIR LINES

AMERICAN AVIATION

The Douglas DC-4, known as the military transport C-54 Skymaster, was one of the most financially successful aircraft in the early post-war years. In 1946, Douglas Aircraft Company introduced an updated version of the Skymaster, the Douglas DC-6, visible in the upper right of this poster. The Skymaster became the Lockheed Constellation's main competitor.

According to a 1947 article in the *Christian Science Monitor,* the Douglas company had learned valuable lessons from its war service and listened constructively to passenger and crew commentary. For example, Douglas engineers made sure that the new airframe would keep temperature consistent throughout the passenger cabin, putting an end to passengers' experiencing "cold feet" and "brows bathed in perspiration." However, in spite of the technological changes that made the DC-6 faster and more comfortable, the airplane was prone to catch on fire. Several deadly crashes in 1947 shocked Americans; the Douglas company chose to ground DC-6s. Nonetheless, even before Douglas modified the DC-6—and especially after the company introduced the DC-7 known as "the last word in piston planes for commercial uses"—airlines around the world lined up to purchase Douglas airliners.

NEW YORK
1947
40 x 25 in.

Your Wings
to and in Korea
KAL
KOREAN AIR LINES
大韓航空
KOREAN AIR LINES

THE 707 JET

"THE WHOOSH OF BRITISH JETS IS LEAVING U.S. PASSENGER-PLANE COMPETITORS farther and farther behind," a reporter for the *Wall Street Journal* fretted in June 1951. The American aircraft industry, however, was reluctant to develop home-grown jet airliners and faced the prospect of losing supremacy in supplying aircraft to airlines flying the prestigious North Atlantic route. The Boeing company decided to do something about the dilemma. Boeing had financed the development of the B-17 bomber and then successfully marketed the airplane to the military during World War II. The company was determined to use the same business plan to develop the U.S.'s first combination jet military transport plane and commercial jet airliner. In 1957 the Boeing 707 was ready. Pan Am president Juan Trippe bought 20—while insisting that Boeing widen the airplane's body to accommodate seating for six passengers in each bank of seats. He also ordered 25 DC-8s from Douglas, a Boeing competitor. The Douglas DC-8 and Boeing 707 became the jets of choice for airlines in Europe, the Americas, and Asia.

Among the reliable customers for American aircraft was the South Korean government. Korean National Airlines (KNA), which began operations in 1948, had used Douglas DC-3s and DC-4s in the 1950s, then purchased a Lockheed Constellation in 1962, the year it went bankrupt. Korean Air Lines (KAL) began flying soon after KNA's demise. When KAL began flying Boeing 707 jets on the Seoul-Los Angeles route in 1972, its marketing department created the poster at left, of a KAL flight attendant holding a Boeing 707 model.

YOUR WINGS TO AND IN KOREA
1972
31 x 21 in.

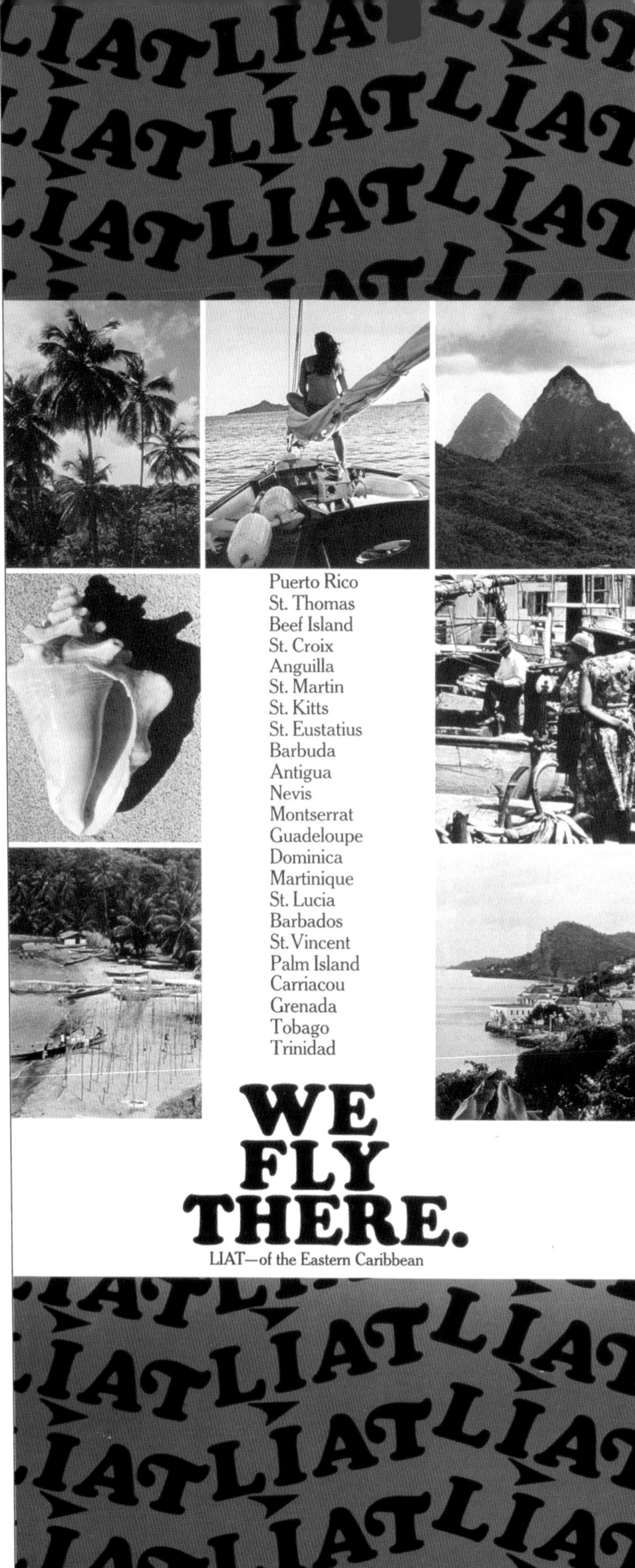
LIAT
Puerto Rico
St. Thomas
Beef Island
St. Croix
Anguilla
St. Martin
St. Kitts
St. Eustatius
Barbuda
Antigua
Nevis
Montserrat
Guadeloupe
Dominica
Martinique
St. Lucia
Barbados
St. Vincent
Palm Island
Carriacou
Grenada
Tobago
Trinidad
WE
FLY
THERE.
LIAT—of the Eastern Caribbean

CHAPTER FIVE

WE FLY THERE

1945–1978

In the first half of the 20th century, wealthy passengers packed carefully to meet weight restrictions as they eagerly prepared to dine and sightsee in style during an airline trip that took several days. They wore their best clothes and remembered their reading glasses, which they needed to examine the detailed strip map the airline provided so they could track every mile of the trip.

Starting in the early 1950s, airlines began introducing tourist-class service. New, lower fares doubled the number of passengers traveling from the United States to Europe by air in 1951-52. Gradually air travel became more common and passengers grew more casual. Throughout the 1960s and early '70s, U.S. airlines flew more passengers on more flights in shorter travel times than ever before. Today, air travelers pack more than they need, dress casually, cover the same route in hours, and watch a movie or sleep to pass the time. But one thing hasn't changed: Air travel still evokes a sense of adventure.

LIAT
1968
38 1/2 x 15 1/16 in.

By the 1950s airlines spent most of their marketing budgets on newspaper and magazine ads. However, posters still played a role in selling air travel. Colorful posters appeared in airports, travel agencies, and airline ticket offices. With the advent of the jet, poster imagery focused less on passengers relaxing in flight or on details of a plane's interior and more on destinations. Posters like the one on page 148 for Leeward Islands Air Transport featured alluring photos of exotic destinations; collages of natural and cultural attractions; and abstract depictions of faraway places. Nouns became verbs as posters cajoled travelers to "jet" to distant lands. Passengers seemed to transform into sophisticated world citizens simply by buying tickets.

Americans had begun a "Ten Billion Dollar Vacation," as reported by the *Chicago Daily Tribune* on June 9, 1946—and they haven't stopped since. More efficient airplanes with greater seating capacity allowed the airlines to decrease fares and attract more passengers. While the International Air Transport Association (IATA) moderated passenger fares for transpacific and transatlantic routes, the Civil Aeronautics Board (CAB) regulated domestic air travel in the U.S. Even though the IATA and CAB were created to keep competition alive and to help the airline business thrive, setting fare rates was subject to "a great deal of bargaining, horse-trading, and tricky maneuvering," according to Max B. Allen, President of the American Association of Travel Agents in

1960. Deregulation of the airlines in 1978 allowed companies to set their own fares without approval of authorities like the IATA or CAB. Until then, airlines still found ways to get around regulations. For instance, offering charter flights allowed them to offer lower fares. Starting in the 1950s, the airlines offered round-trip bargain fares to any group that could legitimately claim to be organized for purposes other than securing a low fare. Charters remained popular into the 1970s. But they weren't always guaranteed. On occasion, the CAB grounded charter flights when investigators deemed the group not sufficiently "group-like"—that is, with no purpose beyond saving money.

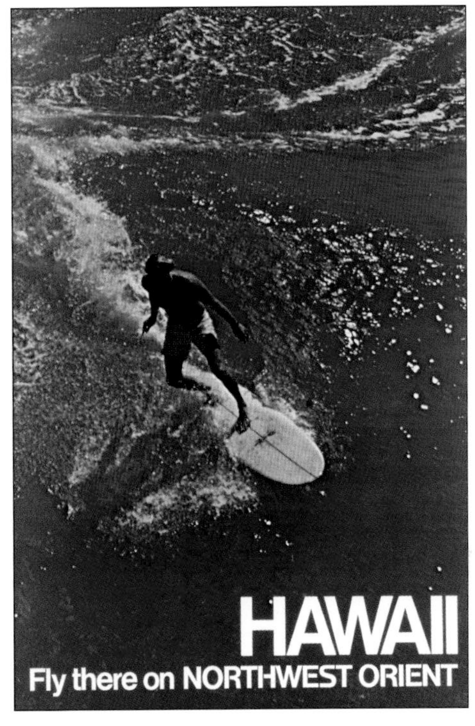
HAWAII
Fly there on NORTHWEST ORIENT

Air travelers wanted to fly to exotic realms such as Hawaii, where record-setting glider pilot "Woody" Parker Brown helped to popularize the ancient sport of surfing in the 1950s.

To compete, airlines like Northwest Orient offered "non-group, group tours." These flights had low fares like charters, but the flights were guaranteed—even to a group whose purpose was unclear, such as Manhattan's Cliff Dwellers, Deviltry, and Diversion Society.

HAWAII
CIRCA 1969
20 x 12 1/2 in.

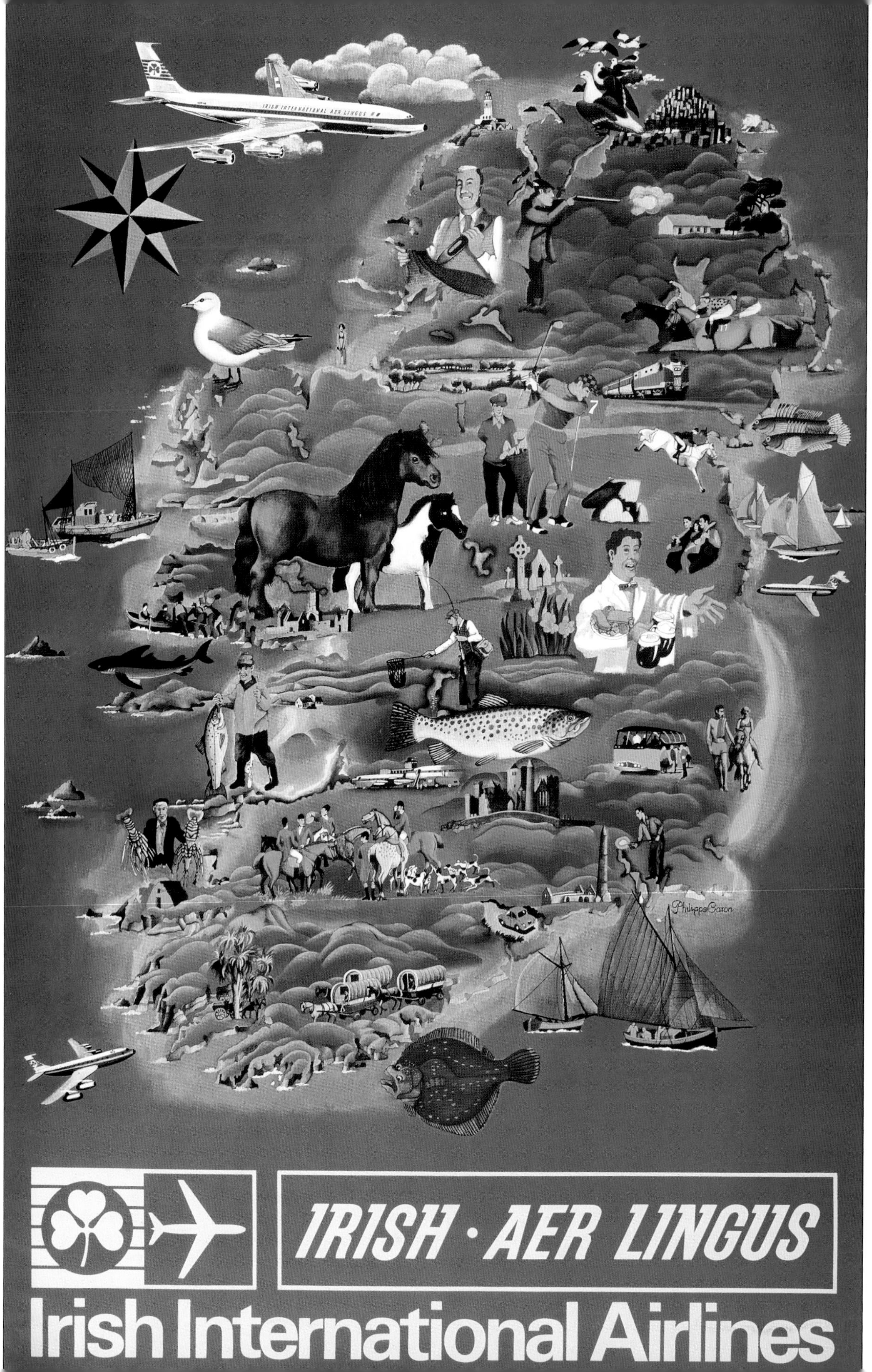

IRISH · AER LINGUS

Irish International Airlines

WHERE IS THERE?

This is modern Ireland, at least according to the poster at left advertising Aer Lingus, Ireland's national airline. Judging from the poster, Ireland, circa 1965, was a major crossroads for North Atlantic jet traffic, as well as a tantalizing destination in its own right. In the early 1950s, the Irish government realized that advertisements promoting Aer Lingus held great potential for reintroducing Ireland to the world and for updating and reshaping international impressions of the Emerald Isle. In 1951, the Irish government sponsored a marketing survey to learn more about the American tourist trade. The resulting report led the designers of advertising campaigns for Aer Lingus to produce graphics that emphasized Ireland's lush landscape, its recreational activities—including fishing and golfing—and its approachable local folk. Cartoons of these themes dot the landscape of this three-dimensional Ireland, which seems to float both in the Irish Sea and in the sky above. The airplanes—including two Boeing 707s flying to Ireland from points west, and a British Aircraft Corporation BAC-111 short-haul jet coming from the east, presumably from London—remind the viewer that Ireland is very much a part of the 20th century and the modern world.

IRISH
CIRCA 1965
39 1/2 x 25 in.

MAIL PASSENGER AND CARGO SERVICES

SP

POLSKA

POLSKIE LINIE LOTNICZE „LOT"

NEW DESTINATIONS

Poland was in ruins after World War II, but its dedication to air power remained strong. When war broke out with the German invasion in 1939, the national carrier LOT went out of business. Many pilots escaped Poland and joined air forces in France and Britain. With the war's end, they returned to Poland to rejuvenate LOT. The Soviet Union had taken control of Poland at the end of the war, and this was evident in the aircraft. Operating Li-2s—Soviet-built Douglas DC-3s—LOT set up offices across Poland. When the poster at left, by Tadeusz Gronowski, was published in 1948, LOT was already offering service from Warsaw to Gdansk in Poland, as well as service to Berlin, Paris, Stockholm, and Prague. Gronowski's 1948 poster shows the "blooming" of postwar Poland (1) in a style reminiscent of folk art and supports the claim of an earlier poster that promoted LOT's role in postwar reconstruction. The powerful airplane (2) suggests that LOT will keep Poland connected with the world. In another poster (3), artist Mieczslaw Teordorczk's imagery reinforces LOT as a symbol of Polish solidarity under Soviet control.

1.

2.

3.

MAIL PASSENGER...; LOT
1948; 1948
39 1/2 x 27 1/2 in.; 39 1/2 x 27 1/2 in.

SMOKE
KUWAIT AIRWAY
THE MIDDLE EAST
SKOL
ACTOR
SUPREME
WRIGLEY'S
HEALTHFUL
DELICIOUS
SATISFYING
LONDON
KUWAIT AIRWAYS CORPORATION

THE JET SET

"So, . . . breakfast-in-New-York-lunch-in-Paris . . . will surely be 'the thing to do' when the jet streamers start soaring next season," reported society columnist Joan Winchell for the *Los Angeles Times* in 1958. Originally, the term "jet set," in American usage, referred to the "sophisticated, well-to-do skiers who go abroad by jet just for skiing vacations in the best-known resorts." Soon, however, journalists, critics, and airline marketing departments considered the jet set those who flew all over the globe to mingle with the rich and famous.

In the 1960s the oil-rich travelers of the Middle East began making their way to European capitals by jet. Many of them traveled with Kuwait Airlines Corporation (KAC), pictured opposite, the 70th airline to open offices in London. In 1938, oil had been discovered in Kuwait, and in the 1940s, the country began exporting its oil and looking to the world outside its borders. In 1954 KAC began flying Douglas DC-3s in the Middle East. In 1963 it inaugurated jet service between Kuwait City, "the Wall Street of the Middle East," and London, using de Havilland Comet 4Cs. KAC filled its planes with entrepreneurs, businessmen, and hip tourists.

LONDON
1964
Size 34 1/4 x 22 in.

VIÑA DEL MAR
CHILE

THE YOUTH MARKET

IN THE MIDDLE OF WINTER 1967, THE *CHICAGO TRIBUNE* RAN AN ADVERTISEment for Saks Fifth Avenue's "Young Elite Salonette." Line drawings of youthful travelers dressed in designer Louis Feraud's "non-stop dress collection" stood near a map of the French Riviera. Saks's intended audience was "the young of all ages, who were en route to the sun places." By the late 1960s, advertising of all kinds reflected the industrial world's growing obsession with the youth culture. Airline marketing often led the pack. No longer did well-dressed, established businessmen and proper matrons represent the airlines. Posters and other marketing materials showed instead young travelers, young stewardesses, or young men and women in exotic settings.

In the poster at left, young men and women in street clothes and swimwear pose with surf boards or guitar, or sprawl on the beach. They appear to be suspended in a universe of their own—youth. This poster was in an ad campaign showing dramatic images of self-important young people at various South American destinations served by Chile's national carrier LAN: A poster advertising Peru turns an out-of-focus shot of a swirling bullfighter into a virile portrait of youth; a poster promoting Argentina depicts young, cosmopolitan diners in a dimly lit steakhouse; another poster touting Chile shows skiers in competition bibs and a young woman in après-ski wear in a lodge rendered surreal by light filtering through the windows. Posters in the campaign sought to convey the exotic destinations awaiting youthful visitors from the north.

VIÑA DEL MAR
1968
33 1/2 x 21 in.

PARIS
JET CLIPPER SERVICE DAILY VIA
PAN AM
WORLD'S MOST EXPERIENCED AIRLINE

THERE: PEOPLE

"The free world has become a neighborhood," according to Pan Am's 1960 annual report. The poster at left advertising Pan Am's daily service between New York and Paris promotes the French city as the ultimate in hospitality, comfortable for persons from all walks of life. Marketing to inexperienced air travelers like middle-class families and students, airlines—especially those flying international routes—often used hand-drawn images or photographs of local citizenry. People smiled, played games, wore clothes distinctive to their country, and made faraway places look familiar enough to entice tentative world travelers to visit.

In the poster, a friendly policeman and a Paris waiter toast each other and perhaps any passenger sensible enough to choose Pan Am. The cityscape in the background hints at broad boulevards, but the stovepipes jutting from the roofline render the scene quaint and welcoming. Although jet service from the U.S. to Paris was only five years old, this 1963 poster uses place rather than airplane to sell tickets. Because jetliners could carry twice as many passengers and fly more economically than propeller-driven airplanes, airlines were able to reduce their fares, making foreign travel accessible to middle-class Americans. Now, along with the jet set, they too could dream of Paris.

PARIS
CIRCA 1963
42 x 28 in.

LAS VEGAS OF THE TROPICS

COUNTRIES IN CENTRAL AMERICA, SOUTH AMERICA, AND THE CARIBBEAN were slower than European and Asian nations to promote tourism in an organized fashion. Violent political unrest, skyrocketing inflation, and attempts to industrialize production left little time for governments south of the U.S. border in the 1950s and 1960s to contemplate the benefits of tourism.

In hopes of bolstering its economy, the Cuban government passed laws in 1955 allowing widespread gambling, and it agreed to provide hefty subsidies to hotel and nightclub builders. Vying for American dollars, Havana hoped to become the "Las Vegas of the tropics," according to one newspaper account. In 1957, Delta Airlines listed Havana as one of its "Millionaire Dream Vacations." After making a $27.61 down payment (the total tour price was $265.55 per person), Delta passengers were on their way to four nights in Cuba.

The poster at right reflects Cuba's focus on its newest tourist attractions. Featuring stereotypes of Cubans whom visitors might encounter in cabarets and casinos, artist William Slattery draws an attractive, if incomplete, picture of the island nation. The hot orange background suggests the blazing, Caribbean sun. A straw hat shades both a cigar-smoking, mustachioed Cubano and an alluring, exotic dancer. In this take on the island nation, a small Douglas DC-7, in the poster's upper right corner, draws attention to Delta Air Lines, which had acquired the Caribbean route in 1953 when it merged with Chicago & Southern Airlines.

DELTA
1957
28 x 22 in.

CUBA
Delta Air Lines

AMERICA
QANTAS
AUSTRALIA'S ROUND-THE-WORLD AIRLINE

THERE: NATURE

Even before Australia's Qantas began using jets, it was busy establishing itself as a "round-the-world-airline." In 1958, flying Lockheed Constellations, Qantas began circling the globe. A flurry of publicity advertised Qantas's new international service and featured a globe-trotting cartoon of a kangaroo. Separate ads showed the kangaroo wearing outfits appropriate to its internatonal destinations, with a well-known tourist site—for instance, Egypt's pyramids—in the background. The ads graced the travel pages of U.S. newspapers from coast to coast.

When Qantas advertised its worldwide destinations to the Australian market, the airline used the formula that had worked in the kangaroo ads. The poster at left attempts to lure Australian travelers to "America." A toothy cartoon squirrel chomping acorns engages the viewer. A line drawing of San Francisco's Golden Gate Bridge represents the destination. The poster was part of a series that included Paris (a poodle and the Eiffel Tower) and London (a bulldog and the Tower of London). Airlines had used nature to sell tickets before destination posters dominated ads; in the 1960s and '70s nature especially resonated with travelers who embraced the environmental movement.

QANTAS
CIRCA 1960
19 1/2 x 14 1/2 in.

FLIGHTS OF FANTASTY

In 1949 the American Chamber of Commerce reported that citizens had spent $500 million in Europe and $90 million in Mexico, but a mere $6 million in Brazil. Historically, trouble obtaining visas, concern over fluctuating currency rates, costly travel fares, and poor amenities had deterred U.S. tourists from traveling to South America. A trip to Rio de Janeiro from the U.S. was arduous. In the 1950s American advertising agencies, travel agents, and others interested in expanding the tourist trade urged Brazilian officials to boost their efforts to cultivate American travelers.

Only in the 1950s did a new government-funded tourist bureau in Brazil take control of advertising its own nation as a destination. Before that, Brazil's image had been in the hands of foreign commercial artists creating ads for companies like Braniff International Airways. Accuracy was not important—hype was. Even the most avid birder would not find a species like the one at right—in South America or anywhere else on Earth. The bird's vibrant pink plumage and dramatic beak steal the show from Rio de Janeiro's famous Sugarloaf mountain (in the poster's background). Whatever tack they took, the goal of airline marketers was to lure U.S. travelers away from Europe to Latin America. Braniff launched fast DC-6 service to Rio, which drastically cut travel time. As one 1950 ad read: "Houston to Rio in 26 hrs. 25 min!" Through the 1950s, Braniff's competitive fares and faster flights inspired many Americans to fly south.

BRANIFF
CIRCA 1949
26 x 20 in.

LATIN AMERICA
BRANIFF
International
AIRWAYS

FLORIDA

EASTERN Air Lines

BEYOND THERE

In an address to Eastern Air Lines' (EAL) marketing department IN 1938, EAL president Eddie Rickenbacker directed, "Don't sell the steak, sell the sizzle." Rickenbacker's employees seem to have taken his advice to heart when they commissioned poster artwork to advertise EAL's new Douglas DC-2 service to Florida. In this 1938 poster, the top end of the thermometer points to Chicago, Eastern Air Lines' Midwest terminus, and its bulb is plunked down right in between EAL's destinations near Florida's east and west coasts. The artwork does not focus on the "steak"—details about the route, the cities served, or specifics of the DC-2—but instead, highlights the "sizzle"—the weather is 76° warm in Florida.

This poster's conceptual presentation of destination was a precursor to jet-era posters, when artists used assemblages of imagery or selected one outstanding illustration to portray a destination. The text accompanying the image was critical to the poster's success. Without the "76° warm," for example, EAL's poster made little sense. As more people flew, the airlines had to work harder to define their own particular brand of sizzle, be it warm climes, exotic surroundings, or enchantment.

FLORIDA
1938
30 x 18 in.

PROMOTING A NEW WORLD VIEW

THROUGHOUT THE 1950S, THE THREAT OF NUCLEAR WEAPONS MADE MANY citizens of the world reconsider technology's benefits. In light of this tension, the theme for Exposition Universelle et Internationale de Bruxelles, also known as Expo '58, was "A World View—A New Humanism." In previous world's fairs, like the Paris Exposition of 1889, the host country had used engineering wonders such as the Eiffel Tower to show off its technological prowess to other nations. By contrast, the 1958 world's fair in Brussels advanced the idea of cooperation in a world community.

The poster at right encouraged Americans traveling to Expo '58 to choose Sabena. At the poster's center, the Atomium, a metal model with nine spheres representing a molecule with nine atoms, showcased Sabena's home base—Brussels, Belgium—and underscored the idea that scientific progress resulting from harnessing the atom could be used for peaceful purposes. The United Nations headquarters, located in New York City and completed in 1953, was a timely symbol of hope for a world community. The poster's cheerful imagery was designed to reassure travelers jittery about the future of the world in a nuclear age. The poster's text reinforces the idea that Sabena's airliner service from New York City to Brussels—with helicopter service from Paris—was more than just a mode of transportation. It was technology bringing a better way of life. Buying a Sabena ticket was buying "fun" in a world trying to put World War II behind it.

SABENA
1957
39 x 24 in

Fun...Brussels
Helicopter...Paris

NEW YORK TO BRUSSELS AND ON TO THE "HEART-OF-PARIS" VIA

BELGIAN *World* AIRLINES

Jet BOAC to Britain

Great place to be happy!

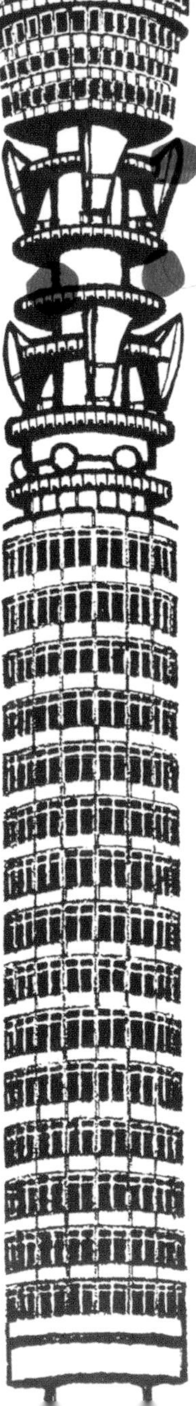

Published by British Travel and printed in Gt. Britain by the Upton Printing Group 93 ENG/69 14

SELLING HAPPINESS

COMMERCIAL ARTISTS WORKING FOR AIRLINES IN THE 1950S AND '60S OFTEN used graphic montages, combining a variety of artistic techniques to convey the onslaught of imagery that modern-day travelers could expect to encounter as they jetted around the world—whether for business or pleasure. The British Overseas Air Corporation's (BOAC) poster at left was created by British Travel, official promoter of United Kingdom tourism, and printed by Upton Printing Group, which also printed album sleeves for popular musicians such as Bob Dylan. A slow-motion photograph, a drawing, and a traditional photograph illustrate the variety of experiences London offered to Americans who wanted to "jet" British.

London was the "place to be"—happy or otherwise—in the late 1960s, and Carnaby Street was said to be the center of all things "mod." After "digging the scene," accompanied perhaps by a fashionably dressed young woman in a "mini" skirt, like the one pictured in the poster, tourists might move on to another of London's modern attractions, the new Post Office Tower. This pillar of concrete and glass, shown at the poster's center, attracted flocks of tourists to its observation decks and revolving restaurant. And when travelers tired of modern London in the "swinging sixties," such traditional tourist spots as Buckingham Palace with the changing of the guard, at poster's right, still beckoned. Other airlines flew between New York and London, but only BOAC promised that Americans could achieve "the pursuit of happiness."

JET BOAC TO BRITAIN
1967
32 3/4 x 25 in.

"FLY NOW, PAY LATER"

IN 1970 *ENDLESS SUMMER* APPEARED ON NATIONAL TELEVISION IN PRIME time. The 1966 cult movie, about two surfers on a quest to find the "perfect wave," appealed to audiences also in search of a dream—a common feeling in the '60s. In 1970 American Airlines launched an "Endless Summer" ad campaign. Anticipating that potential buyers of these vacation packages might include many first-time flyers, American produced detailed timetables and brochures covering many aspects of flying. Reassuring words encouraged the novice traveler: "You're it: the benefactor of a million dreams and plans, participant in an ongoing tribute to the imagination of man."

The sunny words in the poster at right radiate warmth against a deep sea-blue background. Floating above the glowing orb of yellow, orange, and red letters spelling out American Airlines' fun in the sun destinations, the poster's slogan promises unending delight. Responding to the growing number of clients traveling on a budget, the ads noted: "Money is a problem. For almost every traveler." Economy fares and "fly now, pay later" plans allowed vacationers—even those short of cash—to visit the golden beaches of California, Hawaii, and the South Pacific. The airline's credit card in the guise of a "Vacation Card" allowed passengers to "charge it" not only at the ticket counter but also at affiliated hotels, restaurants, and tour offices. It was indeed an endless summer—and a seemingly endless payment program, which added just a "small service charge" to the original cost of the flight.

ENDLESS SUMMER
1970
20 x 15 in.

American Airlines
endless summer

MEXICO
CARIBBEAN
EASTERN USA
WESTERN USA
SO. PACIFIC
HAWAII

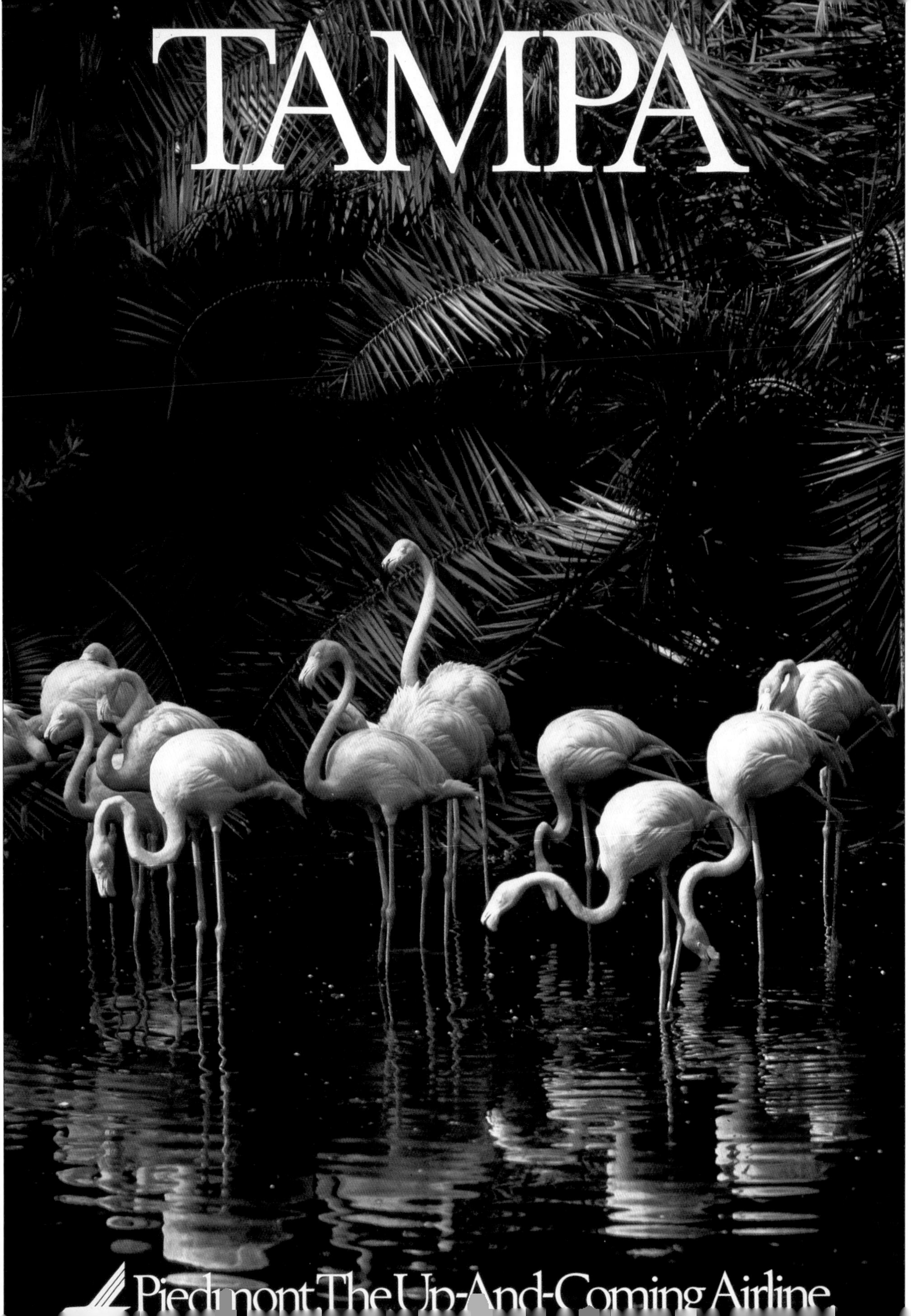
TAMPA
Piedmont. The Up-And-Coming Airline.

FLY NOW!

From the 18th century to the 21st, aeronautical posters have graced the walls of fairgrounds, travel agencies, and airports, their content evolving as the relationship between the aviation industry and its consumers changes. These large and colorful advertisements have played a significant role in introducing and promoting aeronautics, and they have transformed mundane spaces into vibrant and alluring showcases of imagined worlds.

Before World War I, aeronautical posters on billboards urged people to pay to watch balloon ascensions and airplane exhibitions. Between the world wars, aviation posters often brightened the offices of travel agents. Today, in a world of cheap fares and frequent-flyer miles, posters in airports play on the indecision created by seemingly endless choices. They tantalize travelers trudging down jetways: "Next time, choose Bali or Moscow or Spain," or "Take another trip...you know you've got the miles!"

The "endless choices" facing travelers today have resulted in cheaper fares and more flights—but a mostly de-frilled flying experience—as airlines compete for customers. The end of WWII

TAMPA
1978
36 x 24 1/2 in.

marked the beginning of a growth period for the aviation industry. In the United States, small airlines like Piedmont, in the poster on page 176, grew at an unprecedented rate. In those years the U.S. government's Civil Aeronautics Board (CAB) was regulating U.S. domestic airlines—allotting routes and setting ticket fares and schedules. It added cities large and small to Piedmont's route system across the southern U.S. through the 1960s and '70s.

In the late 1970s, U.S. Congress began moving toward deregulation of the commercial airline industry. Deregulation would transfer the CAB's responsibilities to the airlines. Piedmont and other small airlines operating in limited geographic areas feared for their financial well-being if the rules were to change. For example, without CAB control, larger airlines might offer lower fares on Piedmont's routes. Airlines with broader markets had a financial cushion that could absorb potential losses, while Piedmont-size airlines could not lower their fares without drastically cutting into their profit margin. Buy-outs and mergers loomed on the horizon, and Piedmont and other airlines sent representatives to Congress to argue against deregulation. Their lobbying efforts proved unsuccessful. In October 1978, the Airline Deregulation Act became law.

Piedmont survived deregulation fairly well. By comparison, deregulation sped the demise of the small international airline,

"I'll cut fares, but I'll take it on the chin before I'll cut service."
Russell Thayer,
President, Braniff International

This 1978 documentary-style poster featuring Braniff president Russell Thayer sought to reassure passengers and employees that his company was stable. The message reflected Braniff's hopes more accurately than the financial reality.

Braniff. Before deregulation, Braniff had been a colorful, chic place to work. In 1965, it had launched the "End of the Plain Plane" campaign, with influential graphic designer Alexander Girard setting the tone for the airline's corporate identity. His color scheme of seven hues radiated from the airline's planes, advertising materials, airport lounges, and custom-designed hostess uniforms. Meals were prepared by a four-star chef; service was unique.

But Braniff had already expanded beyond its means. With deregulation, it lost sight of its limitations and attempted to compete

I'LL CUT FARES
CIRCA 1978
20 x 28 1/2 in.

Some travel in their minds
Some travel in their hearts
Welcome to the third choice
SAS

with giants like American and United. By 1979 it was spiralling into bankruptcy. The 1978 poster on page 179 sought to reassure Braniff passengers and employees that the company was stable—more a hope than a reality. On May 12, 1982, Braniff ceased flying for the first time; in 1989, under new ownership, the airline flew five more years; in 1989, it filed for final bankruptcy.

The ramifications of deregulation in the U.S. airline industry were many, including the development of new airlines and new alliances. Between 1978 and 1999, when the SAS poster at left was created, international service to and from the U.S. changed remarkably. In 1978, more U.S. airlines began flying the north Atlantic route. Then, in 1979, discount airlines like British-owned Laker Skyways began shuttling travelers at low cost between London and New York City. Airlines used bigger and bigger airplanes, like the Boeing 777, on page 182. In the 1990s, competition along international routes was so fierce that airlines began banding together to share costs and passengers: In 1997, SAS, Air Canada, Lufthansa, Thai Airways International, and United Airlines formed the Star Alliance network. At that time, SAS hired an advertising firm to re-brand its corporate identity. In this poster, the light blue of the SAS logo is intended to convey a happy tone. Airport lounges were outfitted as a "generous Scandinavian home," and while in flight passengers, not the airline, decided when to eat; this

SOME TRAVEL IN THEIR MINDS
1999
39 1/2 x 27 1/2 in.

gave travelers a feeling of comfort and control. In another marketing twist, the poster's dream-inciting slogan—"Some travel in their minds.... Some...in their hearts.... Welcome to the third choice"—was printed onto SAS airplanes. Like the 1970s destination posters in Chapter 5, the SAS campaign seemed to imply that by purchasing an SAS ticket, the traveler purchased a desirable state of being.

The SAS poster campaign ultimately presented air travel as an everyday necessity for conducting business or staying in touch with family. Airlines used this premise for advertising; and by the end of the millennium, flight had become a common commodity. However, after anti-American extremists high-jacked American and United airplanes on September 11, 2001, and flew them into the World Trade Center in New York City, airlines once again had to convince travelers to fly. True, airplanes were safe, comfortable, and reliable; and, true, airlines had years of experience flying passengers on non-stop flights over thousands of miles. But this time airlines faced a new challenge: to convince the public that air travel was safe from terrorists. Since September 11, airlines have managed to do just that. And they continue to add new routes, make new business alliances, and use new aircraft. Passengers, too, have made accommodations to fly in this environment—and, despite ever-increasing security procedures, they still seem poised for air travel, as it beckons them to "Fly now!"

THE MAGNIFICENT SEVENS
CIRCA 1995
18 3/4 x 12 1/2

Boldface indicates posters.

Chapter 1:"Alice Bryant dies," *WashPost*, Sept 9,1954, p. 20; Baden-Powell, B. *Ballooning as a Sport*. W. Blackwood, 1907; "Balloon trips among the clouds," *ChiTrib*, June 5, 1892; Burstyn, Varda. *The Rites of Men*. U Toronto, 1999; Carmona, Michel. *Haussmann*. I.R. Dee, 2002; Croft-Cooke, Rupert. *Circus*. Macmillan, 1977; Crouch, Tom. *The Eagle Aloft*. Smithsonian, 1983; de Fonvielle, Wilfrid. "Gabriel Yon," *L'Aérophile*, March 1894, pp. 63-66; Dollfus, Charles and Henri Bouché. *Histoire de l'Aéronautique*. L'Illustration, 1932; *The Genesis of Flight*. Perpetua, 2000; Gillespie, Richard. "Ballooning in France and Britain," *ISIS*, v. 75, 1984, pp. 249-268; "Goes to the end of the cable," *ChiTrib*, Aug 24, 1892, p. 7; Hardesty, Von. "Aeronautics Comes to Russia," in *NASM Research Report 1985*. Smithsonian, pp. 23-43; "Have left the balloon," *ChiTrib*, Aug 29, 1892, p. 3; Hoage, R.J. and William A. Deiss, eds. *New worlds, new animals*. Johns Hopkins, 1996; Kern, Stephen. *The Culture of Time and Space*. Harvard, 1983; Levin, Miriam R. "Democratic Vistas—Democratic Media," in *French Hist. Stud.*, vol. 18, 1993; Mathews, John Joseph. *The Osages*. U Oklahoma, 1961; "M. Le Blanc wins big city-to-city flight and $47,000 prize," *ChristMon*, Aug 17, 1910, p. 1; "Mrs. Bryant is at home." *BostonGlobe*, Dec 24, 1916, p. 24; "No balloon ascent just yet," *ChiTrib*, Jul 8, 1891, p. 3; "L'Observatoire du Pic du Midi," *La Nature*, no. 99, Apr 24, 1875, p. 321; Rearick, Charles. *Pleasures of the belle époque*. Yale, 1985; Rolt, L.T.C. *The Aeronauts*. Walker, 1966; Speight, George. *A History of the Circus*. Tantivy, 1980; Strasser, Susan. *Satisfaction Guaranteed*. Pantheon, 1989; "They were almost suffocated," *ChiTrib*, Aug 31, 1892, p. 1; Tissandier, Albert. "Le Ballon Captif," *La Nature*, 1891, pp. 63-64 ; — "Necrologie" in *La Nature*, 1904, p. 126; "Took a trip in his balloon," *ChiTrib*, Sept 14, 1892, p. 3; Tucker, Paul Hayes. *The Impressionists at Argenteuil*. Natl. Gal Art, 2000; Weber, Eugen. *France, Fin de Siècle*. Belknap, 1986; — *Peasants into Frenchmen*. Stanford, 1979; "Would not rise to the clouds." *ChiTrib*, Aug. 22, 1892, p. 3.

Chapter 2: "Air-Mail Campaign," *LATimes*, Dec 14, 1932, p. A4; Baedeker, Karl. *Southern Germany Handbook for Travellers*. Karl Baedeker, 1929; Botting, Douglas. *Dr. Eckener's Dream Machine*. Henry Holt, 2001; Burden, William A.M. *The Struggle for Airways in Latin America*. Council on Foreign Relations, 1943; Coolidge, Archibald. "The European reconquest of North Africa," *Am. Hist. Rev.*, v. 17, Jul 1912, pp. 723-734; De Syon, Guillaume. *Zeppelin*. Hopkins, 2002; Doordan, Dennis P. "In the shadow of the fasces," *Design Issues*, v. 13, 1997, pp. 39-52; Fritzsche, Peter. *A Nation of Fliers*. Harvard, 1992; Ghirardo, Diane Yvonne, "Città Fascista," *J of Contemp. Hist.*, v. 31, 1996, pp. 347-372; Hermann, David G. "The Paralysis of Italian Strategy...Italian-Turkish War," *Eng. Hist. Rev.*, v. 104, Apr 1989, pp. 332-356; Hess, Robert L. "Italy and Africa," *J of Afr. Hist.*, v. 4, 1963, pp. 105-126; Homze, Edward L. *Arming the Luftwaffe*. U Nebraska, 1976; "Intitiated 19 Years Ago," *NYT*, May 10, 1929, p. 8; "Items," *ChiTrib*, Sept 2, 1892, p. 3; Le Courbusier. *Aircraft*. Studio, 1935; "Luftfahrtwochenschau," *Luftfahrt*, Feb 20, 1925, p. 54; MacAloon, John J.*The Great Symbol*. U Chicago, 1981; Martin, Percy Alvin. "The Ibero-American Exposition at Seville," *Hispanic-Am. Hist. Rev.*, v. 11, Aug 1931, pp. 373-386; Mosse, George L. *Fallen Soldiers*. Oxford, 1990; "A Mountainous Air Race," *The Aeroplane*, Feb 4, 1925, p. 1; Pisano, Dominick, Tom Dietz, Joanne Gernstein. *Legend, Memory, and the Great War in the Air*. U Washington, 1992; Schiff, Stacy. *St.-Exupéry*. Da Capo, 1996; Segrè, Claudio G. *Italo Balbo*. U California, 1987; "Seville Exposition," *The Atlanta Constitution*, Feb 28, 1929, p. 10; "Spain's big fair delayed,"*NYT*, Feb 7, 1926, p. E4; Stewart, John R. "Manchuria," *Econ. Geog.*, v. 8, Apr 1932, pp. 134-160; Udet, Ernst. *Ace of the Iron Cross*. Doubleday, 1970; van der Linden, F. Robert. *Airlines & Air Mail:* U Kentucky, 2002; von Poturzyn, Fischer. *Junkers and World Aviation*. R. Pflaum, c 1935; Fullam, W.F. "Why every city and town should have a chapter in the National Aeronautic Association," *Aero. Digest*, v. 4, March 3, 1924, p. 187; Woolbert, Robert Gale. "Italian colonial expansion in Africa," *J of Mod. Hist.*, v. 4, Sep 1932, pp. 430-445; "Der Zugspitz-Flug," *Illustrierte Flug-Woche*, Jan 7, 1925, pp. 62-63.

Chapter 3: Allen, Roy. *Pictorial History of KLM*. London: Ian Allan Ltd.,1978; Banning, Gene. *Airlines of Pan American since 1927*. McLean, VA: Paladwr Press,

2001;Bender, Marylin and Selig Altschul. *The Chosen Instrument.* Simon and Schuster, 1982; *The Book of Speed.* Scribner's, 1934; Braden, Donna R. *Leisure and Entertainment in America.* Henry Ford Museum, 1988; Corn, Joseph J. *The Winged Gospel.* Oxford, 1983; Deloria, Philip. *Indians in Unexpected Places.* U Kansas, 2004; D'Harnoncourt, Anne. *Futurism and the International Avant-Garde.* Phil. Mus. Art, 1980; Fraser, Heller, and Chwast. *Japanese Modern.* Chronicle, 1996; Fysh, Hudson. *Qantas Rising.* Angus and Robertson, 1965; Garvey, William and David Fisher. *The Age of Flight.* Pace, 2002; Hill, Roderic. *The Baghdad Air Mail.* Longmans, Green & Co., 1929; Komons, Nick A. *Bonfires to Beacons*: Smithsonian, 1989; Lovegrove, Keith. *Airline Identity, Design and Culture.* teNeues, 2000; Ogburn, William Fielding. *The Social Effects of Aviation.* Houghton Mifflin, 1946; Pudney, John. *The Seven Skies.* Putnam, 1959; R. E. G. Davies. *A History of the World's Airlines.* Oxford, 1964; — *Airlines of Asia since 1920.* Paladwr, 1997; — *Airlines of the United States since 1914.* Smithsonian, 1972; — *British Airways: An Airline and its Aircraft, Vol 1: 1919-1939.* Paladwr, 2005; — *Eastern.* Paladwr, 2003. Sommerfield, Vernon. *Speed, Space, and Time.* Newlson, 1935; Supf, Peter. *Airman's* World. Morrow, 1933; Thornton, Richard. "Japanese Posters," *Design Issues*, v. 6, 1989, pp. 4-14. Tolles, Bryant F. *Resort Hotels of the Adirondacks.* U Press of New England, 2003; Widenheim, Cecilia, ed. *Utopia & Reality.* Yale, 2002; Wood, John Walter. *Airports.* Coward-McCann, 1940; Zega, Michael E. and John E. Gruber. *Travel by Train.* Indiana U, 2002.

Chapter 4:"All DC-6s grounded by fire," *ChiTrib*, Nov 12, 1947, p.1; Brancker, J.W.S. *IATA and What It Does.* Leyden: A.W. Sijthoff, 1977; Davies, R.E.G. *TWA.* Paladwr, 2000; Dobson, Alan P. "The Other Battle" *The Hist. J*, v. 28, Jun 1985, pp. 429-439; Garvey, William and David Fisher. *The Age of Flight.* Pace, 2002; Hagner, Anne. "Women Become Plane Experts Acting as Volunteer 'Spotters," *WashPost*, Apr 1 1943, p. 19; Kim, Samuel. "Korea Is Newest Stop on the Oriental Tour Circuit," *NYT*, Mar 1, 1967, p. XX23; "Korean Air Lines Out to Make Its Mark in International Field," *NYT*, Oct 26, 1969, p. 84; "Scouts Begin Distributing Raid Posters As Mayor Again Urges City to Keep Cool," *NYT*, Dec 27 1941, p. 20; Sloan, Kermit V. "Airlines Get Federal 'Do's and Don'ts,'" *WallStrJ*, Dec 21 1944, p.1; "World Vistas Await Today's Air Travelers," *ChiTrib*, Jan 6, 1946, p. E6; "Youth on the Campus," *ChiTrib*, Aug 30, 1942, p. E2.

Chapter 5 and Epilogue: "Airline Cancels Charter Flight," *WashPost*, Sep 11, 1958, p.C10; Allen, Max B. "Too Much to Fly the Ocean?" *WashPost.* Sep 25, 1960, p. AW3; Bilstein, Roger. *Flight in America, 1900-1983.* Hopkins, 1984; Boczar, Donuta A. "The Polish Poster," *Art Journal*, v. 44, 1984, pp. 16-27; "Delay in accommodations seen for tourist in Argentina," *ChristMon*, Nov 12, 1947, p. 11; Fleming, Douglas K. "Cartographic Strategies for Airline Advertising," *Geog Rev*, v. 74, Jan 1984, pp. 76-93; Gordon, Alistair. *Naked Airport.* Metropolitan, 2004; "Junior Diplomats," *WashPost*, Jul 3, 1960, p. AW14; Ham, Tom. "Delta 'Sell' Rings Bell," *World Airlanes*, July 1958, p. 19; Kahn, Helen L. "Looking Forward and Upward…the 1958 Brussel's World's Fair," *Airlanes,* March 1958, pp. 8-9; King, Linda. "Irish Graphic Design in the 1950s Under the Patronage of Aer Lingus," *CIRCA*, v. 92, Summer 2000, pp. 15-19; "Kuwait Airways," *Air Pictorial*, v. 57, 1995, pp. 298-301; "Kuwait in London," *The Aeroplane*, April 9, 1964, p. 13; *The making of SAS.* A/S Nationaltrykkeriet & Forlagsbokbinderiet, 1973. Nance, John J. *Splash of Colors.* Morrow, 1984; Peach, Robert E. *Four-Seaters to Fan* Jets. The Newcomen Society in North America: 1964; Petzinger, Thomas. *Hard Landing.* New York: Times Books, 1996; Russell, I. Willis. "Among the New Words," *American Speech*, v. 41, May 1966, pp. 137-141; Sampson, Anthony. *Empires of the Sky.* Random House, 1984; "The Sky Ball," *Time*, Sep 5, 1960; "Trans-Atlantic Air Fare Holdup," *ChristMon*, Jun 5, 1963, p. 18; Turpin, John. "The Irish Design Reform Movement of the 1960s," *Design Issues*, v. 3, 1986, pp. 3-21; Wallace, Samuel. "America Begins a 10 Billion Dollar Vacation," *ChiTrib*, Jun 9, 1946, p. E1.

This book would not have been possible had I not had the opportunity to curate the poster collection. Al Bachmeier watched over the posters, offered encouragement, and shared his office space with me. Lillie Gorham has helped me unroll, wrangle, photograph, accession, and inventory the posters for the past 16 years. Paper conservator Diane van der Reyden obtained funding to house the collection. Volunteers Tara Turluk and Beverly Wise helped with the daunting task of processing the collection. Registrars Natalie Rjedkin-Lee and Ellen Folkama facilitated accessioning. Photographers Eric Long, Mark Avino and Carolyn Russo not only got the collection photographed, but also scanned the images for the book. Greg Bryant entered the images into the NASM database. Sam Dargan and Hanna Szczepanowska have expeditiously and with good humor answered all my last minute requests to pull and prepare posters to be photographed.

Every day, my colleagues in the Aeronautics Division at the National Air and Space Museum—Dorothy Cochrane, Roger Conner, Tom Crouch, Dik Daso, Tom Dietz, Von Hardesty, Peter Jakab, Jeremy Kinney, Russ Lee, Suzanne Lewis, Chris Moore, Alex Spencer, Collette Williams—make the NASM an engaging and fun place to work. Ron Davies, Bob van der Linden and Dom Pisano played a particularly influential role in the development of this book: Throughout the past two years, I have spent a good portion of my work day discussing the posters and the history of commercial aviation with them, digging through Ron's airline timetable collection and dossiers, and freely borrowing many of their books. With indulgence and graciousness, they have identified airplanes, read drafts of the book, and mentored me.

William Baxter, Phil Edwards, Carol Heard, Paul McCutcheon, Dan Hagedorn, Alan Janus, Melissa Keiser, Kristine Kaske, Brian Nicklas, and Patti Williams helped find photographs, navigate the vertical files, recommend aviation journals, and order books. Archivists Marie Force (Delta Air Transport Heritage Museum) and Aloha South (National Archives) found the obscure. Michael Beeman, Phil Deloria, Jennifer Forrest, Anne Collins Goodyear, Jennifer Price, Helena Wright, Daqing Yang commented on my poster readings. Marisa Wilairat prepared bibliographies.

Ted Maxwell, Jon Benton, and Scotty O'Connell supported the project in many ways. Patricia Graboske, NASM Publications Officer, sold *Fly Now!* to National Geographic Books. At the NGS, my editor Barbara Brownell Grogan saw the story the posters could tell and made it happen. Art Director Peggy Archambault's beautiful design showcases the posters and highlights the text. Thank you also to Ruth Chamblee, Mike Horenstein, Judy Klein, Kevin Mulroy, Bill O'Donnell, Lauren Pruneski, Barbara Seeber, Susan Straight, and Rob Waymouth.

Thank you Marge and Sheldon London, The McGuirk Center, BE Taxi, Elaine and Marvin Gernstein, and Rachel, Eve, and Matt—you never flagged even when Tuesday kept moving.

—Joanne Gernstein London, 2007

FLY NOW!

BY JOANNE GERNSTEIN LONDON

Published by the National Geographic Society

John M. Fahey, Jr., President and Chief Executive Officer
Gilbert M. Grosvenor, Chairman of the Board
Nina D. Hoffman, Executive Vice President;
President, Books Publishing Group

Prepared by the Book Division

Kevin Mulroy, Senior Vice President and Publisher
Leah Bendavid-Val, Director of Photography Publishing and Illustrations
Marianne R. Koszorus, Director of Design

Barbara Brownell Grogan, Executive Editor
Elizabeth Newhouse, Director of Travel Publishing
Carl Mehler, Director of Maps

Staff for this Edition

Barbara Brownell Grogan, Project Editor
Peggy Archambault, Art Director
Lauren Pruneski, Assistant Editor
Barbara Seeber, Text Editor
Susan Straight, Researcher
Robert Waymouth, Illustrations Specialist
Jennifer Agresta, Indexer
Mike Horenstein, Production Project Manager

Jennifer Thornton, Managing Editor
Gary Colbert, Production Director

Manufacturing and Quality Control

Christopher A. Liedel, Chief Financial Officer
Phillip L. Schlosser, Vice President
John T. Dunn, Technical Director
Vincent P. Ryan, Director
Chris Brown, Director
Maryclare Tracy, Manager

Founded in 1888, the National Geographic Society is one of the largest nonprofit scientific and educational organizations in the world. It reaches more than 285 million people worldwide each month through its official journal, NATIONAL GEOGRAPHIC, and its four other magazines; the National Geographic Channel; television documentaries; radio programs; films; books; videos and DVDs; maps; and interactive media. National Geographic has funded more than 8,000 scientific research projects and supports an education program combating geographic illiteracy.

For more information, please call 1-800-NGS LINE (647-5463) or write to the following address:

National Geographic Society
1145 17th Street N.W.
Washington, D.C. 20036-4688 U.S.A.

Visit us online at www.nationalgeographic.com.

Published by the National Geographic Society
1145 17th St. N.W., Washington, D.C. 20036

First printing, January 2007

The Library of Congress CIP data available upon request.

ISBN 978-1-4262-0088-5

Printed in China